Medical Coding

What It Is and How It Works

Patricia Aalseth, RHIA, CCS

Medical Coding and Documentation Consultant

Albuquerque, New Mexico

JONES & BARTLETT
LEARNING

World Headquarters
Jones & Bartlett Learning
5 Wall Street
Burlington, MA 01803
978-443-5000
info@jblearning.com
www.jblearning.com

Jones & Bartlett Learning books and products are available through most bookstores and online booksellers. To contact Jones & Bartlett Learning directly, call 800-832-0034, fax 978-443-8000, or visit our website, www.jblearning.com.

Substantial discounts on bulk quantities of Jones & Bartlett Learning publications are available to corporations, professional associations, and other qualified organizations. For details and specific discount information, contact the special sales department at Jones & Bartlett Learning via the above contact information or send an email to specialsales@jblearning.com.

Production Credits
Acquisitions Editor: Michael Brown
Production Director: Amy Rose
Production Assistant: Alison Meier
Editorial Assistant: Kylah McNeill
Associate Marketing Manager: Marissa Hederson
Manufacturing Buyer: Therese Connell
Cover Design: Anne Spencer
Composition: Northeast Compositors
Printing and Binding: Malloy, Inc.
Cover Printing: Malloy, Inc.

Library of Congress Cataloging-in-Publication Data
Aalseth, Patricia T.
Medical coding : what it is and how it works / Patricia Aalseth.
   p. ; cm.
Includes bibliographical references and index.
ISBN 0-7637-2739-3
1. Nosology—Code numbers. 2. Clinical medicine—Code numbers.
3. Health insurance claims—Code numbers. I. Title.
[DNLM: 1. Forms and Records Control—standards. 2. Fees and
Charges—standards. 3. Medical Records—standards. 4. Relative
Value Scales. W 80 A112m 2006]
RB115.A27 2006
616'.001'2—dc22
                                    2005017231

ISBN: 978-1-4496-7329-1

6048
Printed in the United States of America
15 14 13 12 11   10 9 8 7 6 5 4 3 2 1

Contents

Why You Need to Know About Medical Coding

Medical coding affects everyone's life, whether we realize it or not. Do these occurrences sound familiar?

- You receive a bill from your doctor's office, for a "balance due" or maybe even "past due."
- You don't remember receiving a previous bill for these charges.
- Your insurance company sends you an "explanation of benefits" to tell you they are not going to pay for anything.
- You are turned down for life insurance because of your "unfavorable history," even though you have always been healthy.
- Your co-insurance portion of the fees for your surgery turns out to be more than the amount you were quoted because "the code is different."

Medical coding influences which medical services are paid, how much is paid, and whether a person is considered a "good risk" for insurance coverage. Quite simply, if there are errors that are not understood, the individual pays too much or, worse, may not be able to obtain health insurance coverage at all. Medical coding can have a fundamental impact on the quality of a person's life.

Medical coding is also a dynamic career choice with growth projected at 36% through 2012.[1] *Medical Coding: What It Is and How It Works* will explain for you just what the title says. In a clear and straightforward manner you will get an overview of the evolu-

---

[1]Bureau of Labor Statistics, U.S. Department of Labor, *Occupational Outlook Handbook, 2004-05 Edition,* Medical Records and Health Information Technicians.
http://www.bls.gov/oco/ocos103.htm

tion of medical coding and all the various coding systems, how they relate and how they function. This book provides information about coding that can help you decide what the profession is all about and if it's the right occupation for you.

For those working in the healthcare field but outside of the coding profession, this book can be of great value as well. Those involved in health care finance, accounting, law, business, medical practice office management, health insurance, etc., should have a basic understanding for how medical coding works. While these individuals won't be performing hands-on coding themselves, it is important for them to understand the basic systems and processes that drive billing, reimbursement, insurance coverage determinations and more. These folks should consider this the ideal coding book for the noncoder.

What Is Medical Coding?

Medical coding is best described as translation. The original language is the medical documentation about the diagnoses and procedures related to a patient. This information is converted, through the coding process, into a series of code numbers that describe the diagnoses or procedures in a standard manner.

Variations in medical language usage can be found in different geographic locales. The sophistication of terms used also varies among different types of medical personnel. Coding the language is a method of grouping medical statements with the same meaning.

> Example: 780.2 Syncope and collapse
>
> Includes: Blackout, fainting, syncope, vasovagal attack

Coded medical information is used for patient care, research, reimbursement, and evaluation of services.

Where to Look for Information

This book is organized into six chapters covering all aspects of medical coding:

Chapter 1: Medical Coding in History

From the Black Death in 16th century London to the multi-billion dollar price tag for the imminent change to ICD-10-CM in 2007, coding has served as a mirror of societal conditions.

Chapter 2: Diagnosis Coding – A Number for Every Disease

There are more than 12,000 different diagnosis codes in ICD-9-CM. This chapter will help you understand the structure and format of I-9 and the process of assigning code numbers to your medical conditions.

Chapter 3: Procedure Coding – Location, Location, Location

Every service you receive as a patient must be enumerated for statistical and billing purposes. The type of procedure, who performs it, and where it is performed determine which coding system is used. This chapter provides information about ICD-9-CM, CPT and HCPCS procedure coding.

Chapter 4: How Codes are Used for Reimbursement

Why is the same procedure paid at a different rate if performed in a doctor's office as opposed to a hospital-based clinic? How can a broken hip affect the hospital's reimbursement for a heart attack patient? This chapter covers payment mechanisms based on coding.

Chapter 5: Coding for Dollars

Tying coding to reimbursement opened the door to potential healthcare organization attempts to "game the system" with fraudulent coding to get more money from payers. What steps were taken to prevent this? What are the current ethical dilemmas of coders today?

Chapter 6: Solving Your Healthcare Coding Problems

What can you do if your insurance claims are turned down due to coding disputes? This chapter provides direction on how to analyze the problem as well as resources you can access by phone, mail, or online.

Chapter 7: Coding as a Career

Popular magazines contain tantalizing ads indicating you can code at home or run your own medical billing service and make mega-bucks. The reality of a coding career does not always involve huge financial return, but coding is guaranteed to be challenging and intriguing. Check out this chapter to see what skills are needed for success.

Appendices

In addition, appendices at the back of the book contain specific national rules and regulations about coding and billing. Take a look at these to see if any problems you are having could be due to someone not following the rules. A single digit error in a diagnosis or procedure code could cost you.

Acknowledgments

Writing a book is a lot more fun if the topic is fascinating. I love medical coding because it is ever-changing but also appeals to my innate need for "a place for everything and everything in its place." The politics of coding reveal national power struggles over which systems will be implemented and who will benefit. Most members of the public haven't a clue how coding affects their health and their pocketbook.

What could offer more drama?

The writing is also a lot easier if the author is spoiled by someone who takes on the other tasks of daily life. My husband, Ed, expanded his culinary repertoire considerably during this third book and our dinners were truly "dining" and not just eating.

Thanks also to everyone at Jones and Bartlett, who are not only helpful but also nice. Publisher Mike Brown encouraged me to do this book and provided ongoing guidance.

As in previous books, my thanks to coders everywhere. We share a profession where we are willing to help each other, which makes it even more worthwhile.

CHAPTER 1

Medical Coding in History

The Black Death

Medical coding in its earliest form started as an attempt to avoid the Black Death. Bubonic plague, caused by the bacteria *yersinia pestis*, arrived in Sicily via ship rats in 1347. It spread rapidly, reaching England in 1348. Almost half the city of London's population of 70,000 died of the disease over the next two years.

Given that life expectancy at the time was about 26 years and about 35% of children died before the age of 6, the Black Death contributed to the increased demise of the already death-ridden populace.

Italian author Giovanni Bocaccio lived through the plague in Florence in 1348. In his book, *The Decameron*, he describes how the Black Death got its name:

"In men and women alike it first betrayed itself by the emergency of certain tumors in the groin or the armpits, some of which grew as large as a common apple . . . The form of the malady began to change, black spots or livid making their appearance in many cases on the arm or the thigh or elsewhere, now few and large, then minute and numerous. These spots were an infallible token of approaching death."[1]

The plague was highly contagious. As soon as people realized that contact with the sick could mean death, they isolated themselves. As Bocaccio describes:

"Citizen avoided citizen, how among neighbors was scarce found any that showed fellow-feeling for another, how kinsfolk held aloof and never met. Fathers and mothers were found to abandon their own children, untended, unvisited, to their fate, as if they had been strangers."[1]

Once the initial scourge was over, isolated outbreaks of plague continued in Europe throughout the next three centuries. It became an increasingly urban disease, due to poor sanitation and crowded living conditions. The Great Plague of 1665 in London killed 25% of the population (Fig. 1-1). It was at this point that the science of epidemiology, the study of epidemics, was born.

Figure 1-1   Plague Doctor. The beak was filled with herbs, thought to ward off the black death

The London Bills of Mortality (Fig. 1-2) were published weekly, and as of 1629 included the cause of death. Information was collected by parish clerks in various geographical areas. In order to determine which areas had the most cases of plague, Londoners purchased copies of the Bills and tracked the spread of the disease from one parish to another in order to avoid it. During one week in 1665, when the total number of London deaths was 8,297, bubonic plague accounted for 7,165 of those deaths.

Causes of death found in the Bills include diseases recognized today, such as jaundice, smallpox, rickets, spotted fever, and plague. Other conditions have creative descriptions like "griping in the guts," "rising of the lights" (croup), "teeth," "king's evil" (tubercular infection), "bit with a mad dog," and "fall from the belfry."

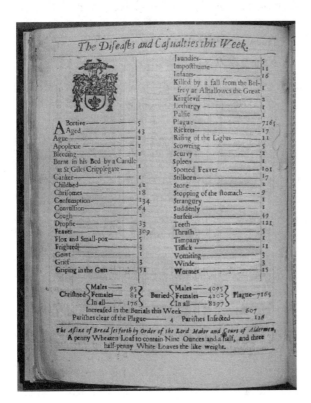

Figure 1-2 London Bills of Mortality, 1665

John Graunt, a London merchant, published *Reflections on the Weekly Bills of Mortality* in 1665. Its central theme was that deaths from plague needed to be examined in the context of all the other causes of mortality in order to understand the effects of all diseases. The sixty disease categories in the Bills constituted the first systematic attempt to analyze the incidence of disease.

During the eighteenth century, additional classifications were authored by Linnaeus in Sweden (*Genera Morborum*, 1763), Bossier de Lacroix in France (*Nosologia Methodica*, 1785), and Cullen in Scotland (*Synopsis Nosologic Methodicae*, 1785). Nosology is the branch of medicine that deals with classification of diseases.

William Farr and the Cholera Studies

As the first medical statistician for the General Register Office of England, Dr. William Farr revamped the Cullen disease classification to standardize the terminology and utilize primary diseases instead of complications. Farr incorporated additional data into his classification, enabling reporting and analysis of factors such as occupation and its effect on cause of death.

Farr's dedication to what he called "hygology," derived from hygiene, was evident in his analysis of the London cholera outbreak of 1849. More than 200 pages of tables, maps, and charts reviewed the possible influence of almost every conceivable death-related factor such as age, sex, rainfall, temperature, and geography. Even day of the week and property value were examined.[2]

The single association consistently present was the inverse relationship between cholera mortality and the elevation of the decedent's residence above the Thames River. Unfortunately this led Farr to the conclusion that the air was more polluted lower by the river, causing the transmission of cholera. He later converted to the water-borne germ theory of disease after studying a second epidemic in 1866, including data about the source of drinking water for those who died.

International List of Causes of Death

The need for a uniform classification of causes of death was recognized at the International Statistical Congress convened in Brussels in 1853. The Congress requested that William Farr prepare a classification for consideration at its next meeting in Paris in 1855. His classification was based primarily on anatomical site and consisted of 138 rubrics.[3] The list was adopted in 1864 and revised at four subsequent Congresses.

Farr died in 1883 and Jacques Bertillon, the chief statistician of the city of Paris, prepared a revised list that was adopted by the International Statistical Institute in 1893. Known as the Bertillon Classification, it was the first standard system actually implemented internationally. The American Public Health Association recommended its use in the United States, Canada, and Mexico by 1898. Delegates from 26 countries adopted the Bertillon Classification in 1900 and subsequent revisions occurred through 1920.

Beyond Death

After Bertillon's death in 1922, interest grew in using the classification to categorize not only causes of mortality, but also causes of morbidity. Morbidity is a diseased state or the incidence of disease in a population. As early as 1928, the Health Organization of the League of Nations published a study defining how the death classification scheme would need to be expanded to accommodate disease tabulation.

Finally, in 1949 at the Sixth Decennial Revision Conference in Paris, the World Health Organization (WHO) approved a comprehensive list for both mortality and morbidity and agreed on international rules for selecting the underlying cause of death. Known as the "Manual of the International Statistical Classification of Diseases, Injuries, and Causes of Death" it is generally referred to as ICD. From this point forward, the use of ICD was expanded, for indexing and retrieval of records and for data concerning the planning and evaluation of health services.

Modern Times

The purpose of the ICD and of WHO sponsorship is to promote international comparability in the collection, classification, processing, and presentation of morbidity and mortality statistics. The United States implemented ICD-1 in 1900 and participated in every revision through ICD-7 until 1968. ICD was used for death classification until the sixth revision, when disease indexing began and ICD was used for both purposes. With the eighth revision, the US developed its own version, known as ICDA-8 or ICD Adapted, due to disagreements over the circulatory section of the international version.

The International Conference for the Ninth Revision was attended by delegations from 46 countries. The classification was being pushed in the direction of more detail by those who wanted to use it for evaluation of medical care or for payment purposes. On the other hand, users in less sophisticated areas did not need the detail in order to evaluate their health care activities. Steps were taken to assure the usefulness of the new revision for all users, and the World Health Assembly adopted ICD 9th revision in May 1976 for implementation effective January 1, 1979. As it did with ICD-8, the US adopted a clinical modification to the international version, and ICD-9-CM (clinical modification) is still in use in this country today.

Reflection of Society

Changes to ICD-9-CM over the years mirror events in American society. The ICD-9-CM Coordination and Maintenance Committee, a joint effort of the National Center for Health Statistics and the Center for Medicare and Medicaid Services, considers code changes yearly. Although it is possible to code any disease using ICD-9-CM, newly identified or newly concerning conditions often fall into an "other" category, and the assignment of new specific codes is necessary to identify and count those disease entities.

1986   New codes assigned for HIV and AIDS. These were previously coded to the "deficiency of cell-mediated immunity" category. By 1986, over 15,000 deaths due to AIDS-related conditions had occurred in the United States and the need for codes was evident.

1989   Lyme disease hit the news, and was assigned an individual code. Although first observed in the US in 1977 near Lyme, Connecticut, its identification as a tick-borne illness caused growing concern throughout the rest of the country.

1991   Kaposi's sarcoma was previously coded in the "other malignant neoplasm" category. Its incidence in AIDS patients made the need to separately identify it more important.

1992   As the popularity of contact lenses grew among Americans, so did the problems associated with them. A new code for corneal disease due to contact lenses was implemented.

1992   What do cooking oil in Spain and L-tryptophan in New Mexico have in common? More than 300 people died in Spain in 1981 due to "toxic oil syndrome," reportedly due to use of contaminated cooking oil. A similar situation occurred in New Mexico in 1989 and on that occasion, L-tryptophan was blamed. It was subsequently banned in the US by the FDA. Both events involved eosinophilia myalgia syndrome, which got a new code in 1992. The Spanish epidemic is now thought to have been caused by organophosphate poisoning from insecticides.[4]

1993   A newly understood connection between some types of HPV, human papillomavirus, and cervical cancer results in the assignment of a separate code for HPV. Investigators have found evidence of HPV in more than 90% of cervical cancers.[5]

1993   With the increasing use of potent antibiotics and other drugs to combat infection, the crafty bugs also developed resistance to those drugs. A series of codes to identify infection with drug-resistant microorganisms was created.

1995   As "couch potatoes" got fatter, the condition of "morbid obesity" got a separate code to distinguish it from other obesity. Morbid obesity is defined as greater than 125% over normal body weight.

1995   Sensational news reports about "flesh-eating disease" described the effects of Group A *streptococcus* manifested as necrotizing fasciitis, a severe soft tissue infection that can result in gangrene. A new code was assigned.

1996   As more premature infants survive due to better medical care, the incidence of RSV bronchiolitis increases. This is due to the respiratory syncytial virus. A new code is assigned for identification purposes.

1996   A sign of the times was the addition of a new code for adult sexual abuse.

1997   Cryptosporidiosis and cyclosporosis got their own codes. These previously rare parasites began showing up more often. An outbreak in Wisconsin where 403,000 people were affected by their drinking water, and additional outbreaks a few years later thought to be caused by imported raspberries, pointed to the need for separate codes.

2002   Although toxic shock syndrome was identified in 1980, it did not receive its own code until 2002. Originally diagnosed in women using high-absorbancy tampons, toxic shock syndrome is now identified in other patients, both male and female, who are infected with *Staph aureus*.

2002   Newly arrived in the US, the mosquito-borne West Nile Virus is assigned its own code.

2002   Codes for the external causes of injury are also part of ICD-9-CM. A new code was needed to identify injuries from paintball guns.

2002   Codes for coronary atherosclerosis had been around for years, but a new code was implemented to identify coronary atherosclerosis <u>in a transplanted heart</u>.

2002   An entire series of codes was added to classify the external causes of injury and death due to terrorism. Among them were codes for terrorism involving biological weapons and terrorism involving destruction of aircraft, including aircraft used as a weapon.

2003   The evening news showed international air travelers wearing surgical masks. The reason—fear of contracting SARS, severe acute respiratory syndrome. This viral illness appeared in southern China in November 2002. Within 8 months, more than 8,000 people had contracted SARS, with almost 800 dying of the disease. SARS was assigned a new diagnosis code in 2003.

2004   "Dermatitis due to other radiation" is added. It includes tanning beds as radiation sources.

As new breakthroughs are made in medical science, and better diagnostic tools developed, additional codes will be required.

What About ICD-10?

ICD-10 represents a radical departure from the previous 100 years of disease classification. Although it is still organized along body systems, it contains about 8,000 causes of death, almost double the 4,000 in ICD-9. It uses 4 to 6-digit alphanumeric codes instead of the 4-digit numeric codes from ICD-9. In the United States, ICD-10 has been used to classify mortality data since 1999, while we continue to use ICD-9-CM for all other purposes, such as billing and morbidity statistics.

The impact of changes in coding systems can be analyzed through a comparability study. This means coding the same deaths twice: once using the old coding system and once using the new coding system. The ratio of new system to old in terms of categories of deaths demonstrates the effect of the coding system change on death rates. In 1979, for example, the data for nephritis, the 11th leading cause of death, had a comparability ratio of 1.74, which means that 74% more deaths occurred from this cause solely due to the change in coding systems.[6]

In 2001, the *Journal of the American Medical Association* published a research letter describing the effect of coding on AIDS mortality statistics in Florida.[7] For 1999, AIDS mortality rose by 6.7% using ICD-10 coding, while it decreased by 6.6% when the same cases were coding using ICD-9. If health services analysts are not aware of these effects, data can be misinterpreted.

Government agencies, health care insurers, and providers are studying the implications of switching to ICD-10-CM. A study by the Robert E. Nolan Company, commissioned by the Blue Cross and Blue Shield Association, estimated a $6 billion to $14 billion price tag on such a change. Other implications cited by the study are:

- A short-term "data fog" due to a lack of data continuity
- Delays and backlogs in payment of claims[8]

If and when a determination is made to change to ICD-10-CM, it will be at least two years from the date of publication of notice in the *Federal Register* before the change is implemented.

References

[1]Bocaccio, Giovanni. *The Decameron.* Translated by JM Rigg. London: the Navarre Society; 1921.

[2]Eyler JM. The changing assessments of John Snow's and William Farr's cholera studies. *Soz.-Präventivmed.* 2001: 46; 225–232.

[3]Scientific Data Documentation International Classification of Diseases—9 (1975). CDC Wonder Website. Available at http://wonder.cdc.gov/wonder/sci_data/codes/icd9/type_txt. Accessed August 7, 2004.

[4]Woffinden B. Cover-up. *The Guardian.* August 25, 2001.

[5]Burk, R. Human Papillomavirus and the Risk of Cervical Cancer. Hospital Practice website. 1999. Available at: www.hosppract.com/issues/1999/11/burk.htm. Accessed August 8, 2004.

[6]*A Guide to State Implementation of ICD-10 for Mortality.* National Center for Health Statistics website. 1998. Available at: ftp://ftp.cdc.gov/pub/Health_Statistics/NCHS/Publications/ICD9_10Con/let.txt. Accessed August 8, 2004.

[7]Grigg. Coding Changes and Apparent HIV/AIDS Mortality Trends in Florida. *JAMA.* 2001: 286; 15:1839.

[8]*Replacing ICD-9-CM with ICD-10-CM and ICD-10-PCS: Challenges, Estimated Costs and Potential Benefits.* 2003. Robert E. Nolan Company website. Available at: http://www.renolan.com. Accessed August 8, 2004.

CHAPTER 2

Diagnosis Coding— A Number for Every Disease

What Is a Diagnosis?

A diagnosis is the identification of a disease from its symptoms. Obviously, the next question is "What is a symptom?" You are the best judge of that because a symptom is a perceptible change in your body or its functions that can indicate disease. Although it is possible to be sick or have a disease and have no symptoms, a symptom is a hint to you that a problem may be occurring. This means you should seek professional help.

When you have a sore throat, that is a symptom. If the sore throat lasts more than a day or two, you will probably visit your doctor to get his or her opinion about the cause of the sore throat. Based on your symptom, the sore throat, and an exam of your physical condition, the doctor may arrive at a diagnosis. There are more than 100 diagnoses that could possibly be the cause of your sore throat. How will the doctor arrive at the correct diagnosis?

Deducing the Diagnosis—History

The first step in the path toward a diagnosis is the **history**. The doctor may ask you:

- How long have you had the sore throat? (duration)
- What part of your throat hurts? (location)
- Is the pain continuous? Better or worse? (timing)
- How does it compare to other sore throats you have had? (severity)
- Do you also have other symptoms? (associated signs and symptoms)
- What are you doing when it hurts? (context)
- How would you describe the pain? (quality)
- What have you done to obtain relief? Did it work? (modifying factors)

These eight categories of questions are known as the **History of Present Illness** (HPI). They constitute a chronological description of your present illness from the first sign or symptom to the present. Once you have responded to these questions, the direction to follow next will usually be clearer to the doctor.

A **Review of Systems** (ROS) is an inventory of body systems obtained through a series of questions seeking to identify signs and/or symptoms that you may be experiencing (Fig. 2-1). Your doctor may give you a check-off form that you fill out yourself in order to get your responses to these questions.

There are fourteen systems that the doctor may review:

Constitutional	Weight, temperature, fatigue, sleep habits, eating habits
Eyes	Vision, use of glasses, pain, blurry vision, halos, redness, tearing, itching

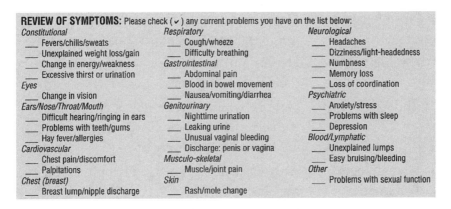

REVIEW OF SYMPTOMS: Please check (✓) any current problems you have on the list below:

Constitutional
___ Fevers/chills/sweats
___ Unexplained weight loss/gain
___ Change in energy/weakness
___ Excessive thirst or urination
Eyes
___ Change in vision
Ears/Nose/Throat/Mouth
___ Difficult hearing/ringing in ears
___ Problems with teeth/gums
___ Hay fever/allergies
Cardiovascular
___ Chest pain/discomfort
___ Palpitations
Chest (breast)
___ Breast lump/nipple discharge

Respiratory
___ Cough/wheeze
___ Difficulty breathing
Gastrointestinal
___ Abdominal pain
___ Blood in bowel movement
___ Nausea/vomiting/diarrhea
Genitourinary
___ Nighttime urination
___ Leaking urine
___ Unusual vaginal bleeding
___ Discharge: penis or vagina
Musculo-skeletal
___ Muscle/joint pain
Skin
___ Rash/mole change

Neurological
___ Headaches
___ Dizziness/light-headedness
___ Numbness
___ Memory loss
___ Loss of coordination
Psychiatric
___ Anxiety/stress
___ Problems with sleep
___ Depression
Blood/Lymphatic
___ Unexplained lumps
___ Easy bruising/bleeding
Other
___ Problems with sexual function

Figure 2-1   "Review of systems" form your doctor may ask you to complete.

Ears, Nose, Mouth, Throat	Pain, hearing loss, infections, nose bleeds, ringing in ears, runny nose, colds, toothaches, sore throat, sores
Cardiovascular	Chest pain, shortness of breath on exertion, murmurs, palpitations, varicose veins, edema, hypertension
Respiratory	Cough, wheezing, bronchitis, color of sputum, spitting up blood
Gastrointestinal	Stomach pain, heartburn, nausea, vomiting, bloating, bowel movements, hemorrhoids, indigestion
Genitourinary	Blood in urine, incontinence, pain on urination, urgency, frequency, urinating at night, dribbling
	Female: menstrual history, sexual history, infections, Pap smears, menopause
	Male: hernias, sexual history, pain, discharge, infections
Musculoskeletal	Joint pain, swelling, redness, limited range of motion, stiffness, deformity
Skin / Breast	Lesions, lumps, sores, bruising, itching, dryness, moles

Neurological	Dizziness, fainting, seizures, falls, numbness, pain, abnormal sensation, vertigo, tremor
Psychiatric	Depression, anxiety, memory loss, sleep problems, nervousness
Endocrine	Hot or cold intolerance, goiter, protruding eyeballs, diabetes, hair distribution, increasing thirst, thyroid disorders
Hematologic / Lymphatic	Anemia, bruising, enlarged lymph nodes, transfusion history
Allergy / Immune	Hay fever, drug or food allergies, sinus problems, HIV status, occupational exposure

The doctor may perform all or part of the review of systems, depending on your presenting problem. The review of systems is intended to identify symptoms you may have forgotten to mention. It also explores and provides support for the doctor's theory about the cause of your symptom. If he feels that the sore throat is due to a respiratory allergy, you can expect to see the respiratory and allergy portions emphasized in the review of systems.

Because there are hereditary or environmental factors that contribute to many diseases, the final part of the history performed by the doctor is known as the **Past / Family / and Social History**.

Past History includes illnesses, surgeries, medications, and allergic reactions. A thorough documentation of past history should include checking by the physician for objective evidence that reported conditions actually existed. Lab results and diagnostic testing reports in your medical record should support the history.

Family History covers any factor within your immediate family that may affect you or the probability that you will have specific conditions, such as cancer, diabetes, heart disease, or other hereditary risk factors. The presence of communicable diseases that are not hereditary can also be important if you are exposed through contact with your family.

Social History encompasses a wide variety of habits, including

- smoking history: how much, how long
- alcohol intake: type, quantity, frequency
- other drug use: type, route, frequency, duration
- sexual activity: gender orientation, birth control, marital status, risk factors
- work history: occupation, risk factors
- hobbies, activities, interests

The information in the social history not only provides additional information relevant to determining the cause of the presenting symptoms but can also facilitate the physician-patient relationship if your doctor knows more about you as a person and not just as a body.

Deducing the Diagnosis—Exam

According to the federal government Center for Medicare and Medicaid Services (CMS), there are 12 different types of physical examinations that can be performed by your doctor. Unless you are seeing a specialist, your doctor will usually perform a "general multi-system examination," including the systems he or she feels are relevant to your presenting problem or symptom.

A few definitions of terms used in describing physical exam procedures include:

- Palpation: Examination by pressing on the surface of the body to feel the organs or tissues underneath.
- Auscultation: Listening to sounds within the body, either by direct application of the ear, or through a stethoscope.

- Percussion: A method of examination by tapping the fingers at various points on the body to determine the position and size of structures beneath the surface.

The officially defined[1] "general multi-system examination" includes:

Constitutional

- Measurement of any 3 of the following 7 vital signs:
  - sitting or standing blood pressure
  - supine blood pressure
  - pulse rate and regularity
  - respiration
  - temperature
  - height
  - weight
- General appearance of the patient (e.g., development, nutrition, body habitus, deformities, attention to grooming)

Eyes

- Inspection of conjunctivae and lids
- Examination of pupils and irises (e.g., reaction to light and accommodation, size and symmetry)
- Ophthalmoscopic examination of optic discs (e.g., size, C/D ratio, appearance) and posterior segments (e.g., vessel changes, exudates, hemorrhages)

Ears, Nose, Mouth, and Throat

- External inspection of ears and nose (e.g., overall appearance, scars, lesions, masses)
- Otoscopic examination of external auditory canals and tympanic membranes

- Assessment of hearing (e.g., whispered voice, finger rub, tuning fork)
- Inspection of nasal mucosa, septum, and turbinates
- Inspection of lips, teeth, and gums
- Examination of oropharynx: oral mucosa, salivary glands, hard and soft palates, tongue, tonsils, and posterior pharynx

Neck

- Examination of neck (e.g., masses, overall appearance, symmetry, tracheal position, crepitus)
- Examination of thyroid (e.g., enlargement, tenderness, mass)

Respiratory

- Assessment of respiratory effort (e.g., intercostals retractions, use of accessory muscles, diaphragmatic movement)
- Percussion of chest (e.g., dullness, flatness, hyperresonance)
- Palpation of chest (e.g., tactile fremitus)
- Auscultation of lungs (e.g., breath sounds, adventitious sounds, rubs)

Cardiovascular

- Palpation of heart (e.g., location, size, thrills)
- Auscultation of heart with notation of abnormal sounds and murmurs
- Examination of
  - carotid arteries (e.g., pulse amplitude, bruits)
  - abdominal aorta (e.g., size, bruits)
  - femoral arteries (e.g., pulse amplitude, bruits)
  - pedal pulses (e.g., pulse amplitude)
  - extremities for edema and/or varicosities

Chest (Breasts)

- Inspection of breasts (e.g., symmetry, nipple discharge)
- Palpation of breasts and axillae (e.g., masses or lumps, tenderness)

Gastrointestinal (Abdomen)

- Examination of abdomen with notation of presence of masses or tenderness
- Examination of liver and spleen
- Examination for presence or absence of hernia
- Examination (when indicated) of anus, perineum, and rectum including sphincter tone, presence of hemorrhoids, rectal masses
- Obtain stool sample for occult blood test when indicated

Genitourinary

Male

- Examination of the scrotal contents (e.g., hydrocele, spermatocele, tenderness of cord, testicular mass)
- Examination of the penis
- Digital rectal examination of prostate gland (e.g., size, symmetry, nodularity, tenderness)

Female

Pelvic examination (with or without specimen collection for smears and cultures) including:

- Examination of external genitalia (e.g., general appearance, hair distribution, lesions) and vagina (e.g., general appearance, estrogen effect, discharge, lesions, pelvic support, cystocele, rectocele)
- Examination of urethra (e.g., masses, tenderness, scarring)

- Examination of bladder (e.g., fullness, masses, tenderness)
- Cervix (e.g., general appearance, lesions, discharge)
- Uterus (e.g., size, contour, position, mobility, tenderness, consistency, descent, or support)
- Adnexa/parametria (e.g., masses, tenderness, organomegaly, nodularity)

Lymphatic

- Palpation of lymph nodes in two or more areas:
- Neck
- Axillae
- Groin
- Other

Musculoskeletal

- Examination of gait and station
- Inspection and/or palpation of digits and nails (e.g., clubbing, cyanosis, inflammatory conditions, petechiae, ischemia, infections, nodes)

Examination of joints, bones, and muscles of one or more of the following six areas: 1) head and neck; 2) spine, ribs, and pelvis; 3) right upper extremity; 4) left upper extremity; 5) right lower extremity; and 6) left lower extremity. The examination of a given area includes:

- Inspection and/or palpation with notation of presence of any misalignment, asymmetry, crepitation, defects, tenderness, masses, effusions
- Assessment of range of motion with notation of any pain, crepitation, or contracture
- Assessment of stability with notation of any dislocation (luxation), subluxation, or laxity

- Assessment of muscle strength and tone (e.g., flaccid, cogwheel, spastic, with notation of any atrophy or abnormal movements

Skin

- Inspection of skin and subcutaneous tissue (e.g., rashes, lesions, ulcers)
- Palpation of skin and subcutaneous tissue (e.g., induration, subcutaneous nodules, tightening)

Neurologic

- Test cranial nerves with notation of any deficit
- Examination of deep tendon reflexes with notation of any pathological reflexes (e.g., Babinski)
- Examination of sensation (e.g., by touch, pin vibration, proprioception)

Psychiatric

- Description of patient's judgment and insight

Brief assessment of mental status including:

- Orientation to time, place, and person
- Recent and remote memory
- Mood and affect (e.g., depression, anxiety, agitation)

Reality Check

You are thinking "My doctor spent 15 minutes with me and didn't do half of this stuff!" You are correct. The extent of the examination will depend on what your doctor needs to examine or measure in order to identify the cause of your sore throat. A likely scenario would be taking your vital signs (done by the nurse), examining your throat, looking at your ears to see if your tympanic membranes are involved, listening to your chest, and possibly palpating your lymph nodes. The doctor will also observe your general appearance for additional signs.

Some of the information obtained during the physical exam is noted solely by observation. The doctor can tell just by looking whether or not you have a rash that might indicate a disease related to a sore throat. Likewise, your ability to walk across the room and climb up on the exam table will provide clues to your gait. The discussion between you and your doctor will yield information about your judgment and insight, and your mental status.

Medical Decision-Making

Now that your doctor knows the history of your sore throat and has examined you, the next step in the process of arriving at a diagnosis is medical decision-making. This involves assessment of the objective data and selection of the most likely cause. It may involve additional diagnostic testing, such as a throat culture to check for bacteria. If you are a smoker or if it is goldenrod season, the doctor may suspect other causes.

In complicated cases with many presenting symptoms, the doctor may use the process of "differential diagnosis," which is weighing the probability of one disease versus another disease as the cause of the patient's symptoms. Sore throat can be caused by bacterial or viral infections, throat irritation or inflammation, allergic reaction, fungal infections, or even just dry air.

Your doctor will make a decision about why your throat is sore and provide a treatment plan that may involve prescription or over-the-counter medications, symptomatic treatment such as gargles, or environmental changes such as a humidifier.

Documenting the Diagnosis

Once the decision-making process is complete, the doctor must document the diagnosis in your medical record. A complete diagnostic statement always includes:

- Site: the physical location
- Etiology: the cause of the condition

For your sore throat, a complete diagnostic statement might be:

- "Strep pharyngitis"
  - Site = pharynx
  - Etiology = streptococcal bacteria

What Number Is My Diagnosis?

Now that you have a diagnosis documented in words by your doctor, it can be converted into a diagnosis code number. In Chapter 1, you learned that the International Classification of Diseases, Revision 9, Clinical Modification (ICD-9-CM) is used in the United States for diagnosis coding. It contains over 12,000 unique codes. This does not mean that each of the more than 100,000 known disease entities has a separate code. When the phrase "diagnosis code" is used, its actual meaning is "diagnosis category code."

An example of a diagnosis category is 790.6: "Other abnormal blood chemistry." This code category includes abnormal blood levels of cobalt, copper, iron, lithium, magnesium, or zinc. Use of 790.6 does not tell you which mineral is abnormal. Nor does it tell you whether the blood level is abnormally low or abnormally high.

A diagnosis code category is analogous to a zip code. The zip code 04558 is for Maine but it covers two towns, New Harbor and Pemaquid. With just the zip code number, it is not possible to positively identify which town is intended.

The translation process known as coding takes the words documented as a diagnosis and converts them into a diagnosis category code number. This is necessary not only for statistical purposes but also because of the variation in the naming conventions for diseases. Regional differences in medical terminology in the United States may result in several different terms for the same disease entity.

Your sore throat diagnosis, "strep pharyngitis," is assigned to a category code number by a two-step process (Fig. 2-2):

1) The main term or noun, "pharyngitis," is located in the alphabetical part of ICD-9-CM, the Index to Diseases; the subterm or adjective "strep" is searched for under "pharyngitis."

2) A category code number, 034.0, is listed next to the entry for "Pharyngitis, streptococcal." In order to assure that this

---

Pharyngitis (acute) (catarrhal) (gangrenous)
        (infective) (malignant) (membranous)
        (phlegmonous) (pneumococcal)
        (pseudomembranous) (simple)
        (staphylococcal) (subacute) (suppurative)
        (ulcerative) (viral) 462
with influenza, flu, or grippe 487.1
aphthous 074.0
atrophic 472.1
chronic 472.1
chlamydial 099.51
coxsackie virus 074.0
diphtheritic (membranous) 032.0
follicular 472.1
fusospirochetal 101
gonococcal 098.6
granular (chronic) 472.1
herpetic 054.79
hypertrophic 472.1
infectional, chronic 472.1
influenzal 487.1
lymphonodular, acute 074.8
septic 034.0
streptococcal 034.0
tuberculous (*see also* Tuberculosis) 012.8
vesicular 074.0

Figure 2.2 Pharyngitis index entries

```
034 Streptococcal sore throat and scarlet fever
    034.0   Streptococcal sore throat
            Septic:               Streptococcal:
            angina                laryngitis
            sore throat           pharyngitis
                                      tonsillitis
            Streptococcal:
            angina
    034.1   Scarlet fever
            Scarlatina
                Excludes parascarlatina (057.8)
```

Figure 2-3   Pharyngitis tabular entries

number is correct, it is necessary to verify the number in the numerical part of ICD-9-CM, known as the Tabular List. The diagnostic terms listed under 034.0 include not only streptococcal pharyngitis, but also streptococcal laryngitis and streptococcal tonsillitis. Thus, the code number 034.0 indicates that the patient had a streptococcal infection of some portion of the throat area, but is not specific to just the pharynx.

How Hard Can This Be?

The two-step coding process described above sounds straightforward: look in the alphabetical index and then verify the number in the tabular list. Why can't this be done by a computer? In fact, most hospitals and other medical facilities now use computerized coding tools called "encoders" to facilitate the coding process. They vary from simple programs that are only replications of the coding books in a computerized format, to sophisticated interactive software that asks all of the questions necessary to arrive at the correct diagnosis category code.

For your sore throat diagnosis, the simple encoder would bring up the list of pharyngitis entries and the coding analyst would have to select "streptococcal" from that list. The sophisticated encoder would find pharyngitis and then ask the user the questions "due to bacteria?" and then "due to which bacteria?" before selecting a code. Branching logic in the sophisticated products assures correct code selection in complex disease entities.

Why can't the computer do it all? The coding process is subject to any number of potential problems that make it essential that a coding analyst, a knowledgeable human being, be involved. Because diagnosis codes are often used to determine reimbursement (see Chapter 4), the coding process is governed by rules that must be followed by any entity submitting a claim for payment by a third party such as a government or private insurance program. Failure to follow these rules can result in the submission of a false claim, which is subject to criminal and civil penalties, including imprisonment and fines.

What can go wrong in the diagnosis coding process?

- Illegible physician handwriting
  What do you think this says?

Figure 2-4   Illegible handwriting

- Illogical physician diagnosis documentation
  "#1) Chest pain secondary to #1"
  "Fractured ear lobe" (not anatomically possible)"
- Lack of physician documentation
- Transcription errors by typist
  "baloney amputation" (should be below-knee amputation)
  "liver birth" (should be live birth)

- Content of the rest of the patient's medical record does not support the diagnosis documented
- Lack of specificity

"anemia" (There are several hundred different types of anemia)

Each of these issues must be resolved before an accurate diagnosis code can be assigned.

What Are the Rules?

The rules for diagnosis coding in the United States are developed and approved by the Cooperating Parties for ICD-9-CM, which include the federal Centers for Medicare and Medicaid Services (CMS), the National Center for Health Statistics, the American Hospital Association, and the American Health Information Management Association. Both ICD-9-CM and the Official Guidelines for Coding and Reporting are in the public domain and may be accessed at no charge on the internet or via public document depository library services.[2]

The rules are 71 pages and consist of:

- Conventions and general coding guidelines
- Chapter-specific guidelines
- Selection of principal diagnosis for inpatients
- Reporting additional diagnoses for inpatients
- Diagnostic coding and reporting guidelines for outpatient services

In addition to the official rules, federal and state government programs such as Medicare and Medicaid promulgate regulations intended to define appropriate code usage or add the weight of law to the guidelines. An example is the Medicare transmittal defining for its contractors the appropriate rules for ICD-9-CM coding for diagnostic tests.[3] This transmittal was issued because of concerns about contractors in different geographic locations inconsistently interpreting the official guidelines.

General Coding Guidelines

These guidelines tell coding analysts the basic information they need to code correctly, based on physician documentation.

A. Use both the alphabetic index and the tabular list when locating and assigning a code.

B. Locate each term in the alphabetic index and verify the code selected in the tabular list. Read and be guided by instructional notations.

C. Valid diagnosis codes may have 3, 4, or 5 digits. A 3- or 4-digit code may only be used if it is not further subdivided.

Example: "481 Pneumococcal pneumonia" may be used because it is not further subdivided. "482 Other bacterial pneumonia" may not be used because it is further subdivided into 4 and 5 digit codes.

D. Codes that describe symptoms and signs, as opposed to diagnoses, are acceptable if a definitive diagnosis has not been established by the physician.

Example: 780.2 Syncope (fainting) is a symptom code. It may be used if the physician does not identify and document a diagnosis responsible for the fainting.

E. Signs and symptoms that are an integral part of a disease process should not be assigned as additional codes.

Example: Fluid overload is integral to congestive heart failure and would not be coded separately.

F. Signs and symptoms that may not be associated routinely with a disease process should be coded when present.

G. Some single conditions may require more than one code for a full description. Generally, one code is for the etiology and one for the manifestation of the disease. Instructions, such as "code first," "use additional code," "code, if applicable, any causal condition first," guide the coder. Additional situations requiring more than one code are related to late effects, complications, and obstetrical cases.

H. When a condition is described as both acute and chronic, code both.

Example: Acute sinusitis is 461.9.

Chronic sinusitis is 473.9.

Both codes would be used for "Acute and chronic sinusitis."

I. Combination codes are single codes used for a combination of two diagnoses, or a diagnosis with an associated manifestation or complication. Do not use multiple codes if a combination code describes all of the elements.

Example: Acute cholecystitis is 575.0.

Chronic cholecystitis is 575.11.

Acute and chronic cholecystitis is 575.12.

Only 575.12 would be used to describe both.

J. A late effect is the residual effect after the acute phase of an illness or injury has terminated. There is no time limit as to when a late effect code can be used. The residual condition is coded first.

Example: "907.2 Late effect of spinal cord injury," could be used as an additional code if a patient was being seen for neurogenic bladder.

Abbreviations present in ICD-9-CM are:

- NEC Not elsewhere classifiable. Detail in medical record is specific, but a specific code is not available. Same as "other specified."

- NOS Not otherwise specified. Same as unspecified. Information in medical record is not sufficient to assign a more specific code.

- X Used as a placeholder in codes where additional information is needed to assign a specific 4th or 5th digit.

Notes used in ICD-9-CM are:

Includes: Defines or gives examples of the content of the category.

Excludes: Terms excluded are to be coded elsewhere. Used in the case of logical inconsistencies such as a congenital versus acquired condition.

Inclusion terms: Synonyms of the code title. May be supplemented by additional terms found only in the alphabetical index.

What Is the Structure of the Diagnosis Codes?

How is the diagnosis system set up to handle the thousands of coding categories in a logical fashion? The 17 chapters in the Classification of Diseases and Injuries are divided along two major schemes:

- Anatomic system chapters, such as Diseases of the Digestive System, or

- Disease or condition categories, such as Neoplasms, where all neoplasms are found, regardless of anatomic location.

Chapter Title	Code Range
Infectious and Parasitic Diseases	001.0–139.8
Neoplasms	140.0–239.9
Endocrine, Nutritional and Metabolic Diseases, and Immunity Disorders	240.0–279.9
Diseases of the Blood and Blood-Forming Organs	280.0–289.9
Mental Disorders	290.0–319

Chapter Title	Code Range
Nervous System and Sense Organs	320.0–389.9
Diseases of the Circulatory System	390–459.9
Diseases of the Respiratory System	460–519.9
Diseases of the Digestive System	520.0–579.9
Diseases of the Genitourinary System	580.0–629.9
Complications of Pregnancy, Childbirth and the Puerperium	630–677
Diseases of the Skin and Subcutaneous Tissue	680.0–709.9
Diseases of the Musculoskeletal System and Connective Tissue	710.0–739.9
Congenital Anomalies	740.0–759.9
Certain Conditions Originating in the Perinatal Period	760.0–779.9
Symptoms, Signs and Ill-Defined Conditions	780.01–799.9
Injury and Poisoning	800.00–999.9

Within each ICD-9-CM chapter and section, there are categories that are arranged in mostly logical fashion, either by body site or by the cause or etiology. Subcategories are arranged the same way, with the last subcategory generally being used for "other" diagnoses that may be nonspecific. See Appendix A for a list of all ICD-9-CM categories. You may use this list to get a general idea of where your diagnoses occur in the coding scheme.

Two additional classifications are used in diagnosis coding to indicate situations beyond the disease itself:

- Supplementary Classification of Factors Influencing Health Status and Contact with Health Services (V codes): Used in situations where a person who does not have an illness or injury utilizes health services, such as a vaccination. Code range is V01.0 through V83.89.

- Supplementary Classification of External Causes of Injury and Poisoning (E codes): Used to indicate the causes of accidents and intentional acts resulting in injury. For example, a burn caused by a firecracker would have an E code for "accident caused by explosive material, fireworks." Code range is E800.0 through E999.1.

Which Diagnosis Is Listed First?

The sequencing of diagnosis codes is intimately linked to reimbursement (see Chapter 4) and thus is also defined by official rules.

Inpatient

The Uniform Hospital Discharge Data Set or UHDDS applies to diagnosis sequencing for inpatient, short-term, acute care, and long-term care hospital records. It has been in use since 1985 and defines the principal diagnosis as "that condition established after study to be chiefly responsible for occasioning the admission of the patient to the hospital for care."[4] According to this definition, if you are admitted to the hospital because of chest pain, but fall out of bed and break your hip, the chest pain will still be your principal diagnosis, even if you end up staying an extra two weeks to have your hip repaired.

Sequencing rules for inpatients are:

- Do not use a symptom or sign as the principal diagnosis if a definitive diagnosis has been established.

- If there are two or more interrelated conditions that could each meet the definition of principal diagnosis, either may be sequenced first.

- Comparative/contrasting conditions documented as "either/or" are sequenced according to the circumstances of the admission.

- If a symptom is followed by comparative/contrasting conditions, all are coded, with the symptom first.

- Even if the original treatment plan is not carried out, follow the definition for principal diagnosis.

- If admission is for treatment of a complication, the complication code is sequenced first.

- If the diagnosis is documented as "probable," "suspected," "likely," "questionable," "rule out," the condition is coded as if it existed.

Note: the last rule varies significantly from that for outpatients (see below). The UHDDS Guidelines are found in Appendix H.

Outpatient and Physician Office

Because the UHDDS does not apply to outpatients, the selection of the first diagnosis is governed by the ICD-9-CM Official Guidelines. The "first-listed diagnosis" is defined as "the diagnosis, condition, problem, or other reason for encounter/visit shown in the medical record to be chiefly responsible for the services provided."[5] Additional rules for outpatient sequencing are:

- Do not code diagnoses documented as "probable," "suspected," "questionable," "rule out," or "working diagnosis." Rather, code the condition to the highest degree of certainty for that encounter/visit, such as signs, symptoms, abnormal test results, or other reason for the visit. Note: This rule for outpatient sequencing differs significantly from the last rule noted previously for inpatients.

- For patients receiving diagnostic services only, sequence first the diagnosis, condition, problem, or other reason shown to be responsible for the service.

- For patients receiving therapeutic services only, code first the diagnosis responsible for the service. An exception to this rule occurs if the encounter is for chemotherapy, radiation therapy, or rehab, in which case the V code for the service is listed first and the diagnosis second.

- For pre-op exams, use the appropriate V code, followed by the condition necessitating the surgery.

- For ambulatory surgery, use the diagnosis for which the surgery was performed. If the post-op diagnosis differs from the pre-op, select the post-op for coding.

- For routine prenatal visits when no complications are present, use the V codes for supervision of pregnancy.

What's in Each Diagnosis Chapter?

As each ICD-9-CM diagnosis chapter is discussed, any applicable coding rules from the Official Guidelines will be included.

Chapter 1—Infectious and Parasitic Diseases (001-139)

The diseases in this chapter are those considered to be communicable, either from human to human or from another host, such as a mosquito, to humans. Parasites are organisms that live in or feed on humans, such as worms. This chapter is the realm of public health departments across the nation that monitor and try to prevent outbreaks of communicable diseases.

The structure of this chapter is based on the organism causing the condition to be coded, but can also be grouped according to the primary body system affected. An example is the intestinal infectious diseases, a section that includes cholera, typhoid, salmonella, shigellosis, other bacterial food poisoning, amebiasis, other protozoal intestinal diseases, intestinal infections due to other organisms, and ill-defined intestinal infections.

As new organisms are identified and new outbreaks of infectious diseases occur, additional codes are added frequently to this chapter. Some of the conditions in this chapter represent diseases thought to be eradicated, such as smallpox. The last known case was in 1977. However, small quantities of the virus exist in research laboratories, and the potential for accidental exposure is still present, so it is necessary to retain the code for possible future use. For some conditions, vaccines have been developed for prevention but diseases occur in other age groups who have not been vaccinated. An example is whooping cough in adults.

In some coding categories, lots of detailed codes are available but the usual medical record documentation is too scanty to allow their use. An example is tuberculosis, where fifth digits are based on the method by which the mycobacterium infection was confirmed.

Specific official coding guidelines for conditions in this chapter include:

HIV (Human Immunodeficiency Virus Infections)

Reason for Encounter	Use Code
Treatment of HIV-related condition, AIDS	042
Treatment of unrelated condition	Code for condition plus 042
Patient is "HIV-positive" without symptoms	V08
Inconclusive HIV test, no diagnosis	795.71
HIV infection in pregnancy	647.6X plus 042
Asymptomatic HIV during pregnancy	647.6X plus V08
HIV testing	V73.89
Receive results of HIV testing	V65.44

The physician's diagnostic statement that the patient is HIV positive or has an HIV-related illness is sufficient to code. Current documentation of positive serology or culture is not required.

Septicemia, Systemic Inflammatory Response Syndrome (SIRS) Sepsis, Severe Sepsis, and Septic Shock

Reason for Encounter	Use Code
Urosepsis (urinary tract infection)	599.0 plus code for organism if known
Bacteremia (bacteria in blood)	790.7
Septicemia (systemic disease associated with presence of microorganisms in blood)	038.0–038.9
Sepsis (SIRS due to infection)	038.9 plus 995.91
Severe sepsis (SIRS due to infection that advances to organ dysfunction)	038.X plus 995.92 or 995.94 plus codes for organ dysfunctions
SIRS (systemic inflammatory response syndrome—clinical response to insult, infection, or trauma, includes systemic inflammation, temp change, rapid heart rate and respiration, elevated white count)	995.9X used as a secondary diagnosis
Septic shock (septicemia with shock)	Code for initiating trauma or infection, plus 995.92 or 995.94 plus 785.52

Either the term sepsis or SIRS must be documented to assign a code from subcategory 995.9.

Late Effects of Infectious or Parasitic Diseases

Reason for Encounter	Use Code
Late effect of tuberculosis	Code for residual condition plus 137.X
Late effect of polio (this includes post-polio syndrome)	Code for residual condition plus 138
Late effect of other infectious or parasitic disease	Code for residual condition plus 139.X

Related to the infectious disease codes are the V09 codes for infection with drug-resistant organisms, which would be used as additional codes secondary to the infection code.

V Codes Related to Infectious Diseases

Reason for Encounter	Use Code
Exposure to a communicable disease	V01.X
Carrier of an infectious disease	V02.XX
Need for vaccination	V03.XX–V06.X
Need for isolation	V07.0
Screening for infectious diseases	V73.XX–V75.9
Lab work for suspected disease	V71.9

Chapter 2—Neoplasms (140-239)

The word "neoplasm" means new growth. From a coding perspective, there are four types of neoplasms:

- Malignant

   In common usage, the term "cancer" is used to describe a malignant neoplasm. These new growths are usually invasive, spreading to the lymph system and to distant sites in the body (metastases).

   ◦ Primary—malignant neoplasm in the site where it originated

   ◦ Secondary—malignant neoplasm in the site it has metastasized to, or spread to

○ In Situ—carcinoma cells that are still confined to the original site and are undergoing malignant changes

- Benign

  Although benign neoplasms do not spread to other sites, their growth may cause problems due to size, putting extra pressure on nearby structures.

- Uncertain behavior

  For some tumors, a decision cannot be made about whether they are benign or malignant, even upon pathology examination.

- Unspecified nature

  This category is for neoplasm documentation that is not specific enough to determine the behavior.

Specific official coding guidelines for conditions in this chapter include:

Neoplasms

Reason for Encounter	Use Code
Treatment of the primary malignancy (not chemo or radiation)	Code for malignant neoplasm of primary site
Treatment of a secondary (metastatic) site only	Code for malignant neoplasm of secondary site
Treatment of anemia associated with malignancy	Code for anemia plus code for malignancy
Treatment of dehydration due to malignancy or therapy	Code for dehydration plus code for malignancy
Treatment of complication of surgery for an intestinal malignancy	Code for complication
Chemotherapy	V58.11 plus code for malignancy
Radiation therapy	V58.0 plus code for malignancy
Follow-up after cancer treatment, with no evidence of recurrence	V67.1 or V67.2 plus V10.XX code for history of malignant neoplasm
Follow-up with evidence of recurrence	Code for neoplasm
Prophylactic organ removal to prevent occurrence of cancer	V50.4X

Care must be taken when the term "metastatic" is used. It can mean either a primary neoplasm that is spreading, such as a laryngeal tumor that has spread to a cervical lymph node. However, "metastatic" can also be documented by the physician to refer to the metastatic site, such as "metastatic cancer, lymph node."

In assigning neoplasm codes, it is essential that the search begin by looking for the morphologic type (name such as carcinoma, glioma, leiomyoma). This is necessary in order to learn whether the neoplasm is malignant, benign, or other, Once this information is in hand, the search moves to the anatomic site.

Chapter 3—Endocrine, Nutritional, and Metabolic Immunity (240-279)

Endocrine glands secrete hormones directly into the bloodstream. The hormones travel to target organs and are often involved with metabolism, which is the chemical process taking place in living tissues, necessary for the maintenance of the organism. A disease state in an endocrine gland can affect not only the target organ but also related systems. This is demonstrated clearly in the complications of diabetes, involving the kidneys, eyes, nerves, and peripheral vascular system.

The endocrine diseases are organized according to the involved endocrine gland: thyroid, pancreas, parathyroid, pituitary, thymus, adrenal, ovarian, and testicular. The nutritional deficiencies are arranged with malnutrition first, followed by the various vitamin and mineral deficiencies. The metabolic disorders follow the substance being metabolized, such as carbohydrates, proteins, lipids. Additional codes for obesity and immunity deficiencies round out the chapter.

There are no official coding guidelines for this chapter of ICD-9-CM. However, there are concepts related to diabetes that affect coding:

Diabetes Mellitus

Reason for Encounter	Use Code
Treatment of Type I diabetes (absolute deficiency of insulin, juvenile onset). Patients with Type I diabetes always require insulin. As of 10/04, the term "insulin-dependent" is no longer used for coding purposes.	250.X1
Treatment of Type II diabetes (resistance to the effects of insulin, adult onset). Patients with Type II diabetes may or may not require insulin. As of 10/04 the term "non-insulin dependent" is no longer used for coding purposes.	250.X0
Complications of diabetes, such as retinopathy, nephropathy, ketoacidosis, coma, ulcer	250.XX depending on the complication and the type of DM plus additional code for the complication
Dietary counseling	V65.3 plus code for diabetes
Diabetes complicating pregnancy	648.0X
Gestational diabetes	648.8X
Infant of a diabetic mother syndrome	775.0
Neonatal diabetes	775.1
Abnormal glucose tolerance test	790.22

Physician documentation of the type of diabetes is essential. It cannot be assumed that all patients who are on insulin are Type I.

Another problematic diagnosis category is thyroid disorders. If your physician does not enunciate clearly or spell the words when dictating, you could end up with the wrong disease. "Hypo-" and "hyper-" thyroidism sound very similar.

Chapter 4—Diseases of the Blood and Blood-Forming Organs (280-289)

Anemia accounts for the largest portion of this chapter. In order to classify it correctly, detailed documentation is needed. There are 35 different code categories for anemia. Deficiency anemias can be due to blood loss, malabsorption of nutrients, or nutritional deficiencies. Hemolytic anemias, in which red cells are destroyed at an abnormal rate, can be hereditary or acquired. Aplastic anemia occurs when the bone marrow fails to produce the normal amount of blood components. The other major part of this chapter is coagulation defects—when the blood does not clot properly. The most well-known condition of this type is hemophilia. Diseases of the white cells, with the exception of leukemia, are also in this chapter. Leukemia is in the neoplasms chapter.

Since the lymph system and the spleen are also related to blood, they are included in this chapter.

There are no official coding guidelines related to this chapter.

V Codes Related to Blood Disorders

Reason for Encounter	Use Code
Blood donor	V59.0X
Blood-alcohol test	V70.4
Routine lab work	V72.60
Lab work for suspected disorder	V71.9
Hemophilia genetic carrier	V83.0X
Pre-op lab work	V72.63 plus code for condition requiring surgery

Chapter 5—Mental Disorders (290-319)

The American Psychiatric Association has defined a mental disorder as "a clinically significant behavioral or psychological syndrome or pattern that occurs in an individual and that is associated with present distress (a painful symptom) or disability (impairment in one or more important areas of functioning) or with a significantly increased risk of suffering death, pain or disability."[6] The Association's *Diagnostic and Statistical Manual of Mental Disorders, 4th edition* (known as DSM-IV) is a tool to assist clinicians in diagnosis of mental disorders. It consists of an index of mental illnesses accompanied by listings of possible symptoms and diagnostic criteria. This classification is not used for healthcare billing purposes, although almost all of the code numbers in this scheme agree with those in ICD-9-CM.

More than other specialties, psychiatry is likely to have codable services that are rendered by providers other than physicians. Clinical psychologists, counselors, social workers, and therapists participate in services for psychiatric patients. Psychiatry is also heavily involved with the legal system because of the need for involuntary treatment of some patients and the use of mental illness as a defense in legal cases.

This chapter is divided into three main sections:

- Psychoses (290-299)
- Neurotic Disorders, Personality Disorders, and other Nonpsychotic Mental Disorders (300-316)
- Mental Retardation (317-319)

As life expectancy increases and the aging population expands, the incidence of organic psychotic conditions (290-294) increases. These are physical conditions that cause a decrease in mental function. Psychosis is a loss of contact with reality, typically including delusions (false ideas about what is taking place or who one is) and hallucinations (seeing or hearing things that aren't there). The organic psychoses include senile dementias, alcoholic psychoses, drug-related psychoses, and other organic mental disorders such as acute confusional state. Other psychoses not defined as organic include schizophrenia, affective disorders, paranoid states, and childhood psychoses.

The nonpsychotic mental disorders include personality disorders, neuroses, sexual disorders, alcohol and drug abuse and dependence, sleep disorders, eating disorders, stress and adjustment reactions, conduct disorders, developmental delays, and childhood emotional disorders. Nonpsychotic mental disorders due to organic brain damage are also in this section.

Mental retardation has its own section; the codes are based on the intellectual quotient (IQ) of the patient.

There are no official coding guidelines for this chapter. Patients with mental disorders may be seen for services under a number of circumstances:

Mental Disorders

Reason for Encounter	Use Code
Treatment of mental illness	Code for mental illness
Treatment of mental illness associated with a physical condition	Code for mental illness plus code for the associated physical condition
Treatment of mental illness due to an underlying disease	Code for the underlying disease plus code for the mental illness
Counseling for marital, partner, or parent-child problems (without psychiatric diagnosis)	V61.1X–V61.3
Counseling for other psychosocial circumstances, such as work environment, legal issues, refusal of treatment (without psychiatric diagnosis)	V62.X
Substance abuse counseling	V65.42
Follow-up exam following completion of psychotherapy	V67.3
Lifestyle issues such as gambling, high-risk sexual behavior	V69.2-V69.9
Exam for medico-legal reasons	V70.4
Observation for suspected mental condition	V71.0X
Pre-operative psychological exam	V72.85 plus code for condition requiring surgery

Chapter 6—Nervous System and Sense Organs (320-389)

The nervous system is responsible for sensory and motor activities, for behavior, and for regulating the internal organs. Sensory functions are those of vision, smell, hearing, taste, touch, and proprioception (the body's awareness of itself). Motor functions are those of movements, such as swallowing and heartbeat.

Coding nervous systems conditions requires knowledge of the location or site of the condition. The central nervous system is the brain and the spinal cord. The peripheral nervous system includes all other nervous system elements, such as the facial nerves, cranial nerves, and nerves in the extremities.

Central nervous system diseases include infections, such as encephalitis and meningitis, and degenerative disorders, such as Alzheimer's disease, Parkinson's disease, and other types of tremor. Some of these diseases are hereditary and some are acquired. Multiple sclerosis, cerebral palsy, migraine, and epilepsy are other CNS conditions.

Hemiplegia (paralysis of one side of the body) can be a current condition or the residual effect of a previous occurrence, such as a stroke. A fifth digit is used with codes for hemiplegia to indicate whether the patient's dominant or nondominant side is affected.

The peripheral nervous system is involved in many common conditions, such as carpal tunnel syndrome, peripheral neuropathy, Bell's palsy, and hereditary conditions such as muscular dystrophy.

The section on eye disorders includes not only codes for all types of eye diseases, but also a method for coding visual impairment such as low vision or blindness. A defined scale of visual acuity levels is used to define the level of impairment. Although codes exist in the ear section for hearing loss, it is classified or coded based only on the type of loss and not on the degree of loss.

Cataracts and glaucoma are common in aging populations. Glaucoma is a rise in the pressure inside the eye, which can restrict blood flow. Most types of glaucoma are due to blockage of the flow of aqueous, the fluid inside the eye. Cataracts occur most often in the elderly, but can also occur in other age groups, due to trauma, drugs, radiation, and other causes.

Otitis (ear inflammation or infection) is one of the most common childhood illnesses. There are 21 different codes for acute and chronic forms of otitis media or middle ear infection. The physician must document very specifically to assure correct code assignment. There are no official coding guidelines for the section on nervous system and sense organ diseases. Patients may need health services for a variety of reasons:

Nervous System and Sense Organs

Reason for Encounter	Use Code
Treatment of a nervous system or sense organ condition	Code for the condition
Treatment of a nervous system or sense organ condition associated with another condition	Code for the nervous/sensory condition plus additional code for the other condition
Treatment of a nervous system or sense organ condition due to an underlying disease	Code for the underlying disease plus code for the nervous/sensory condition
Fitting or adjustment of artificial eye prosthesis	V52.2
Fitting or adjustment of glasses or contact lenses	V53.1
Fitting or adjustment of hearing aid	V53.2
Fitting or adjustment of devices related to nervous system, such as neuropacer	V53.0X
Rehab	V57.1 Physical therapy
	V57.2X Occupational or vocational therapy
	V57.4 Orthoptics plus code for the underlying condition being treated
Surgery follow-up	V67.00
Routine eye exam	V72.0
Routine hearing exam	V72.19

Chapter 7—Diseases of the Circulatory System (390-459)

The circulatory system covers the heart, arteries, veins, and capillaries. Its purpose is to obtain oxygen from the lungs, distribute it to tissues via blood flow, and release carbon dioxide, the waste product of the body's metabolism or energy consumption. The heart is the pump that makes the circulatory system work.

The lymph system, which produces and distributes immune cells, is also included in this chapter. Congenital heart conditions are found in Chapter 14, while circulatory conditions related to pregnancy are in Chapter 11.

Interestingly, this chapter starts with an infectious disease. Rheumatic fever is a febrile inflammatory condition that may occur after infection with group A strep. It can cause arthritis and other joint symptoms, but its primary complication is carditis and damage to the heart, particularly the valves.

Hypertension, or high blood pressure, is defined as blood pressure consistently greater than 140 systolic or 90 diastolic. Systolic is the top number in your blood pressure and represents the pressure when the heart beats. Diastolic is the bottom number and represents the pressure when the heart rests. Hypertension can involve the heart and the kidney if not treated successfully.

Heart attack, or myocardial infarction, is another group of codes in this chapter. It is a form of ischemic heart disease, in which the supply of blood to the heart is blocked, usually due to arteriosclerosis.

Varicose veins, thrombophlebitis, hemorrhoids, and deep vein thrombosis are the most commonly seen conditions of the arteries and veins.

This chapter has a number of official coding rules:

Circulatory System

Reason for Encounter	Use Code
Hypertension, essential or NOS	401.X Do not use codes for benign or malignant unless specified
Hypertension with heart disease—causal relationship stated (due to hypertension) or implied (hypertensive)	402.XX Use additional code from 428 if patient has heart failure

Circulatory System (continued)

Reason for Encounter	Use Code
Hypertension with heart disease—causal relationship not documented	Code heart disease and hypertension separately
Hypertensive renal disease with chronic renal failure	403.XX Causal statement not required
Hypertensive heart and renal disease—causal statement for heart disease present	404.XX Use an additional code for 428 if the patient has heart failure
Hypertensive cerebrovascular disease	Code from 430-438 plus hypertension code
Hypertensive retinopathy	362.11 plus code from 401-405
Secondary hypertension	Code for underlying cause and code from 405 for hypertension
Transient hypertension, or elevated blood pressure without hypertension diagnosis	796.2
Hypertension stated as controlled or uncontrolled	Appropriate code from 401-405
Late effect of cerebrovascular disease, such as neurological deficits	Code for deficit plus 438

Because diagnosis sequencing is related to reimbursement, CMS peer review organizations have developed additional guidelines for the circulatory chapter:

Reason for Encounter	Sequence
Angina due to coronary artery disease	CAD Code for angina
Unstable angina resulting in acute MI	MI No code for angina
Acute MI, postinfarction angina	MI Code for angina
Chest pain, no cause identified	Chest pain code
Chest pain, cause identified	Code for cause
Congestive heart failure with fluid overload, dilated cardiomyopathy, pleural effusion, or respiratory failure	CHF
Cerebrovascular accident (stroke) with positive diagnostic tests and symptoms still occurring after 24 hours	CVA—434.91
Presentation as stroke / CVA but diagnostic tests are negative and symptoms are resolved within 24 hours	TIA (transient ischemic attack) 435.9

Patients with circulatory disorders may also be seen for other reasons:

Circulatory System

Reason for Encounter	Use Code
Fitting or adjustment of cardiac device such as pacemaker	V53.3X
Cardiac rehab	V57.89
Aftercare following surgery	V58.73
Therapeutic drug monitoring (anticoagulant use)	V58.83 plus V58.61
Surgical follow-up	V67.00
Pre-operative cardiovascular exam	V72.81 plus code for condition requiring surgery
Observation for suspected cardiovascular disease	V71.1

Chapter 8—Diseases of the Respiratory System (460-519)

Starting at the top, the respiratory system consists of the nasal cavity and sinuses, the mouth, throat (pharynx and larynx), bronchi, and lungs. Its function is to bring in air, containing oxygen, and to release carbon dioxide. The oxygen passes into the blood in an exchange process that takes place in the alveoli of the lungs; carbon dioxide passes from the blood into the lungs and is exhaled.

Code categories in this chapter are arranged starting with upper system infections, other upper diseases, pneumonia, obstructive diseases, lung diseases due to external agents, and other respiratory diseases.

The categories for lung diseases due to external agents read like a list of poor labor conditions from American history: coal workers' pneumoconiosis (black lung disease), mushroom workers' lung, farmers' lung, cheese washers' lung, bauxite fibrosis, chemical bronchitis.

The official coding guidelines for this chapter are used in conjuction with sequencing guidelines developed by Medicare peer review organizations because diagnosis coding affects reimbursement.

Respiratory System

Reason for Encounter	Sequence
Pneumonia, unspecified cause	486
Pneumonia, known cause. Physician must document bacterial or viral cause.	480.X–483.X
Pneumonia in infectious disease classified elsewhere	Code for underlying disease, then 484.1–484.8
Lobar pneumonia. The same term can be used for two different diseases.	486 for site (lobe) 481 for pneumococcal (lobar is synonym)
Chronic obstructive pulmonary disease (COPD) exacerbation, cause not identified	491.21
COPD with respiratory distress or insufficiency	COPD code only
COPD with respiratory failure	Respiratory failure code
Respiratory failure due to respiratory cause	Respiratory failure
Respiratory failure due to nonrespiratory condition, chronic	Respiratory failure
Respiratory failure due to nonrespiratory condition, acute or acute exacerbation	Acute non-respiratory condition
Asthma—The physician must document cause and whether exacerbation is present.	493.0X–493.9X
Pleural effusion with CHF	CHF. Use pleural effusion as secondary code if drained.
Pleural effusion with other cause	Sequence according to conditions of admission

Patients with pulmonary diseases may be seen for other reasons:

Reason for Encounter	Use Code
Pneumovax vaccination	V03.82
Desensitization to allergens	V07.1
Attention to tracheostomy	V55.0
Aftercare following surgery to respiratory system	V58.74
Therapeutic drug monitoring	V58.83
Routine chest x-ray	V72.6
Pre-op respiratory exam	V72.82 plus code for condition requiring surgery

Chapter 9—Diseases of the Digestive System (520-579)

The length of the average digestive system is an amazing 27 or 28 feet! The basic function of this system is to prepare food for absorption, by mechanical and chemical methods. In mechanical digestion, food is ground, torn, chewed, shaken, and mixed with saliva and stomach juices. In the small intestine, the dissolved food particles are mixed with enzymes and are absorbed through the lining of the intestine into the intestinal-hepatic portal venous system where nutrients move into the bloodstream and are delivered to the rest of the body.

Coding categories for the digestive system are arranged according to the physical site of the disease: teeth, gums, jaw, salivary glands, oral soft tissues, tongue, esophagus, stomach, duodenum, appendix, abdominal cavity, intestine, colon, rectum, anus, liver, gallbladder, and pancreas. The pancreas serves an endocrine function by producing insulin, but it is also considered a digestive organ because it secretes enzymes that aid in digestion of proteins, fats, and carbohydrates.

Gastrointestinal infections that are contagious are located in the infectious disease chapter, while gastrointestinal neoplasms are located in that chapter.

There are no official coding guidelines for the digestive system disease chapter. Patients with these diseases may be seen for:

Digestive System

Reason for Encounter	Use Code
Attention to gastrostomy	V55.1
Attention to ileostomy	V55.2
Attention to colostomy	V55.3
Attention to other artificial opening of gastrointestinal tract	V55.4
Aftercare following surgery of the teeth, oral cavity, and digestive system	V58.75
Surgery follow-up	V67.00

Digestive System (continued)

Reason for Encounter	Use Code
Screening for malignant neoplasm, rectum	V76.41
Screening for malignant neoplasm, intestine	V76.50
Screening for malignant neoplasm, colon	V76.51
Screening for malignant neoplasm, small intestine	V76.52

Because reimbursement is tied to diagnosis sequencing, some of the CMS peer review organizations have developed additional guidelines.

One of the common conditions in the gastrointestinal (GI) tract is bleeding. If the cause of the bleeding is identified, the code for that condition, with hemorrhage, is used. A code from category 578, gastrointestinal hemorrhage, is used only when the bleeding is documented but no bleeding site or cause is identified. The most common causes of upper GI bleeding are ulcers and diverticular disease.

Chapter 10—Diseases of the Genitourinary System (580-629)

The urinary portion of this system is comprised of the kidneys, ureters (tubes connecting the kidneys to the bladder), bladder, and urethra (tube from bladder to the outside). Its function is to eliminate waste products and also to maintain chemical and body water balances. If it is a hot day and you do not drink enough water, the volume of your urine will decrease as the kidneys work to maintain the appropriate internal balance.

The genital portion of this system includes not only what is normally thought of as genitalia, but also the breasts. The male genital portion covers the prostate, penis, testes, spermatic cord, and seminal vesicles. The female portion includes the ovaries, fallopian tubes, uterus, vagina, cervix, clitoris, labia, and vulva. Reproduction and preservation of the human species are the tasks of these systems.

Kidney failure may lead to the need for the patient to undergo dialysis. In this procedure, a dialysis machine serves as a substitute for the kidney, filtering out salts and urea wastes into a solution that can be discarded.

The presence of stones, or calculi, can occur in the kidney, ureters, bladder, or urethra. Often painful, these stones are usually formed of calcium or uric acid. They can prevent the passage of urine if located in the wrong spot. The flow of urine can also be affected by conditions in the prostate because the urethra passes through the prostate on its way to the penis. Enlargement of the prostate is found in more than 40% of men over the age of 70. For coding purposes, the cause of the hypertrophy must be specified.

Breast disorders, with the exception of neoplasms, are also located in this chapter. They are not restricted to use in female patients. Breast neoplasms are found in ICD-9-CM Chapter 2.

Coding for female genital tract conditions is organized along anatomical divisions, with a few functional sections at the end of the chapter addressing menstrual disorders, menopause, and infertility.

There are no official coding guidelines for this chapter. However, patients may be seen for these conditions for a variety of reasons:

Genitourinary System

Reason for Encounter	Use Code
Contact or exposure to venereal diseases	V01.6
Contact or exposure to HIV	V01.79
Exposure to potentially hazardous body fluids	V15.85
Sterilization	V25.2
Prescription of oral contraceptives	V25.01
Fitting of diaphragm	V25.02
Insertion of IUD	V25.11
Reversal of sterilization	V26.0
Artificial insemination	V26.1

Genitourinary System (continued)

Reason for Encounter	Use Code
Fertility testing	V26.21
Prophylactic organ removal	V50.41 Breast
	V50.42 Ovary
	V50.49 Testes
Breast augmentation or reduction	V50.1
Routine circumcision	V50.2
Fitting or adjustment, urinary catheter	V53.6
Renal dialysis	V56.0
Peritoneal dialysis	V56.8
Aftercare following surgery to genitourinary system	V58.76
Kidney donor	V59.4
HIV counseling	V65.44
Sexually transmitted disease counseling	V65.45
Surgery follow-up	V67.00
Paternity testing	V70.4
Observation following alleged rape	V71.5
Routine GYN exam	V72.31
Screening mammogram	V76.11
Screening breast exam	V76.19
Screening for malignant neoplasm	V76.47 vagina
	V76.2 cervix
	V76.44 prostate
	V76.45 testis
	V76.46 ovary
Dietary counseling	V65.3

Chapter 11—Complications of Pregnancy, Childbirth, and the Puerperium (630-677)

This chapter is the most complex within ICD-9-CM in terms of the official guidelines. It contains codes for many conditions that are classified elsewhere, but which are coded within this chapter if the patient is pregnant or has delivered and is within the puerperium, defined as 42 days after delivery.

In addition to pregnancy, abortion is also part of this chapter, since it is considered an outcome of pregnancy, whether spontaneous, legally induced, illegally induced, or unspecified. Although the chapter title references "complications," normal pregnancies are also in this chapter.

Many of the codes in this chapter utilize fifth digits that indicate the outcome or the nature of the condition or complication:

0 = unspecified as to episode of care or not applicable

1 = delivered this episode, with or without mention of antepartum complication

2 = delivered this episode, with mention of postpartum complication

3 = antepartum condition or complication

4 = postpartum condition or complication

The guidelines for this chapter are extensive:

Pregnancy, Childbirth, and the Puerperium

Reason for Encounter	Use Code
Other condition, pregnancy is incidental	Code for other condition plus V22.2
Prenatal outpatient visits for patients with high-risk pregnancies	Code from category V23
Prenatal visit, routine, no complications present	V22. 0 or V22.1
	Do not use another chapter 11 code with these
Normal vaginal delivery (full term, single healthy infant, no complications during delivery) (Inpatient)	650 plus V27.0 for outcome of delivery
	Do **not** use any other chapter 11 code with 650
Other Delivery (Inpatient)	Main circumstances or complication of delivery
C-section delivery (Inpatient)	Reason a C-section was performed
Complication of pregnancy but no delivery occurs (Inpatient)	Code corresponding to the principal complication of the pregnancy
HIV-related illness during pregnancy	647.6X plus 042 plus code for the HIV-related illness
Fetal condition affecting the management of the mother	Code from 655 or 656 categories
Delivery outside hospital, admitted for routine postpartum care, no complications	V24.0
Late effect of complication of pregnancy, childbirth or the puerperium	Sequela code plus 677

Abortion coding includes fifth digits that indicate the stage of the abortion:

0 = unspecified stage

1 = incomplete (all products of conception have not been expelled from the uterus)

2 = complete (all products of conception have been expelled from the uterus prior to the episode of care)

The following official coding guidelines relate to abortion:

Abortion

Reason for Encounter	Use Code
Treatment of spontaneous abortion (no instrumentation or chemical intervention)	Category 634
Legally induced abortion (elective, termination of pregnancy)	Category 635
Treatment after illegally induced abortion (not performed in accordance with state law)	Category 636
Treatment after unspecified abortion	Category 637
Failed attempted abortion (elective abortion procedure has failed to evacuate the fetus and the patient is still pregnant)	Category 638
Complications following abortion, ectopic and molar pregnancies	Category 639
Complication of pregnancy leading to an abortion	Abortion code plus code from 640-648 or 651-657 for the complication
Attempted abortion with liveborn fetus	644.21 plus V27 code for outcome of delivery
Retained products of conception following a spontaneous or legally induced abortion	Code from category 634 with a fifth digit of 1
Missed abortion (fetal death prior to 22 completed weeks gestation, with retained fetus)	632
Ectopic pregnancy (outside the uterus)	Category 633

Patients in the antepartum or postpartum period may be seen for a variety of reasons:

Reason for Encounter	Use Code
Postpartum care immediately after delivery	V24.0
Postpartum care of lactating mother	V24.1
Routine postpartum follow-up	V24.2
Genetic counseling and advice	V26.33
Antenatal screening	Category V28
Multiparity	V61.5
Illegitimate pregnancy	V61.6
Other unwanted pregnancy	V61.7
Dietary counseling	V65.3
Pregnancy testing, pregnancy unconfirmed	V72.40

Chapter 12—Diseases of the Skin and Subcutaneous Tissue (680-709)

The skin is part of what is known as the integument. This protective covering keeps the deeper tissues from drying out and protects them from injury and infection. The epidermis is the outer layer. It contains nerve endings, hair shafts, sweat gland openings, and several layers of cells. As old cells are worn away, they are replaced. The dermis is the next layer, consisting of hair follicles, sebaceous glands, sweat glands, nerves, arteries, veins, and connective tissue. The superficial fascia is the deepest layer of integument. It is the layer between the skin and the muscles or bones.

Coding for skin conditions is divided into categories for infections, inflammatory conditions, and other diseases. In addition to the hair follicles, sebaceous and sweat glands, the nails are an important appendage to the skin. They grow through proliferation of cells at their roots, pushing the new nail growth out.

This chapter has a few differences from the regular coding schemes. Sunburn is in this chapter, not in the injury chapter that contains other types of burns. A number of skin infections, despite the fact that they may be contagious, such as impetigo, are in this chapter instead of Chapter 1 of ICD-9-CM. Acute lymphadenitis is in this chapter, while chronic lymphadenitis is in the blood chapter.

Physician documentation is extremely important in correctly classifying dermatitis. There are a number of causes and it is not possible to code the condition correctly without specific information.

As the population ages, a common skin condition among those with limited mobility is the ulcer. Decubitus ulcers, also known as bedsores, result from pressure on skin points from the patient's body weight and the resulting lack of blood circulation. Other types of skin ulcers can result from hypertension, diabetes, or phlebitis, an inflammation of the veins.

There are no official coding guidelines for the skin chapter, but patients with skin conditions can be seen for a number of reasons:

Skin and Subcutaneous Tissue

Reason for Encounter	Use Code
Hair transplant	V50.0
Face lift	V50.1
Aftercare involving the use of plastic surgery	V51.X
Dressing change	V58.3X
Aftercare following surgery of the skin and subcutaneous tissue	V58.77
Skin donor	V59.1
Surgery follow-up	V67.00
Screening for skin cancer	V76.43
Suture removal	V58.32

Chapter 13—Diseases of the Musculoskeletal System and Connective Tissue (710-739)

This chapter covers the bones, joints, muscles, and fascia. Many of the code categories in this chapter use fifth digits to denote the anatomic site of the coded condition:

0 = site unspecified

1 = shoulder region

2 = upper arm

3 = forearm

4 = hand

5 = pelvic region and thigh

6 = lower leg

7 = ankle and foot

8 = other specified sites (head, neck, ribs, skull, trunk, vertebra)

9 = multiple sites

The adult body contains more than 200 bones and approximately 600 muscles, so it is important to be specific in coding diseases and conditions of these systems. Because they are made primarily of mineral salts such as calcium and are more durable than other body tissues, bones are frequently the only thing left when remains must be examined in conjunction with scientific or legal investigation. The length of various individual bones can be used to estimate the height of a person, while the structure of the pelvis can differentiate between males and females.

Three types of muscles produce movement within the body. Cardiac muscle in the heart wall, and smooth muscle in the stomach, intestine, and blood vessel, are known as involuntary muscles. They work without conscious direction from you and you do not have conscious control over them. Your heart continues to beat without your telling it to do so; you are not able to prevent the smooth muscle in your stomach from contracting when you vomit. Skeletal muscles, those attached to the bones, are voluntary because they are under your control. Muscles make up more than 40% of your body weight.

Other parts of the musculoskeletal system are ligaments, which connect bone to bone, and tendons, which connect muscle to bone. Fascia is the covering of the muscles, which also contains blood vessels and nerves.

Joints are points at which bones are connected to each other. The shape of the joint determines how it will be able to move:

- Ball and socket joints, such as the hip and shoulder joints, permit movement in basically three directions
- Hinge joints, like the elbow and ankle, permit movement that is mostly restricted to one plane
- Pivot joints, like the skull on the 1st vertebra in the neck, allow for rotation of the head from side to side.
- Sutures between the bones of the skull are joints but are immovable
- Cartilaginous joints, such as the discs between the vertebra, allow for only partial movement
- Gliding joints occur where two flat surfaces of bone glide across each other

Damage to joints, tendons, and ligaments occurs with aging, trauma, and with inappropriate use.

There are no official coding guidelines for the musculoskeletal system chapter, but patients with these conditions may be seen for a variety of reasons:

Musculoskeletal System

Reason for Encounter	Use Code
Joint disorder in conditions classified elsewhere	Code for underlying disease plus code for current arthropathy
Bone infections	Code for current condition plus code for organism, if known
Fitting and adjustment of artificial prosthesis	Arm V52.0
	Leg V52.1
Fitting and adjustment of orthopedic devices such as braces, casts, shoes	V53.7
Fitting and adjustment of wheelchair	V53.8
Aftercare involving removal of internal fixation devices such as pins, screws, rods	V54.01–V54.09
Aftercare for healing traumatic fracture	V54.10–V54.19
Aftercare for healing pathologic fracture	V54.20–V54.29
Aftercare following joint replacement	V54.81
Physical therapy	V57.1
Occupational therapy	V57.21
Orthotic training (artificial limbs)	V57.81
Suture removal	V58.32
Aftercare following surgery for injury and trauma	V58.43
Aftercare following surgery of musculo-skeletal system, not elsewhere classified	V58.78
Bone donor	V59.2
Bone marrow donor	V59.3
Exercise counseling	V65.41
Observation following accident	At work V71.3
	Other V71.4
Screening for osteoporosis	V82.81 plus code for hormone replacement or menopause
X-ray	Code for findings, or if no findings, code for reason for performing x-ray
Pre-operative exams	V72.81 EKG
	V72.82 Chest x-ray
	V72.83 Other
	Plus code for reason for surgery

Chapter 14—Congenital Anomalies (740-759)

Congenital anomalies are structural defects present at birth. The common term for these conditions is birth defects. A major anomaly is apparent at birth in 3 to 4% of newborns; up to 7.5% of children manifest a congenital defect by the time they are five years old.[8] They may be due to genetics or teratogens, which are chemical or radiation in nature and affect normal fetal development. Approximately 4,000 congenital anomalies have been identified.[9]

For coding purposes, it is important that the physician define a condition as congenital if it is a condition that could be either congenital or acquired. For example spina bifida, which is a lack of closure of the spinal cord's bony encasement, can only be congenital. However, obstruction of the intestine can be either congenital or acquired. For conditions where either possibility exists, the coder cannot make the assumption that the condition is congenital just because the patient is very young.

Likewise, it may be appropriate to use a code for a congenital condition for an older patient. It is legitimate to do this as long as the condition still exists and the patient is receiving treatment for it.

New medical terminology may result in the use of a term before a code exists. Syndromes are often eponymic, which means they are named after a person. An example of both is Partington's syndrome. It is named after an Australian geneticist and describes X-linked mental retardation. Since there is no code, it would be necessary to code the chromosome deficiency and the mental retardation separately.

The official coding guidelines for the congenital anomaly chapter help code patients seen under many circumstances.

Congenital Anomalies

Reason for Encounter	Use Code
Congenital anomaly treated during episode of care when birth occurred	V30-39 for liveborn infant plus code for the congenital anomaly
Infant admitted after birth episode for treatment of anomaly	Code for the anomaly
Contraceptive management (adult with genetic concerns who does not want to reproduce)	V25 category
Genetic counseling and testing	V26.3 category
Observation of newborn for suspected genetic condition	V29.3
Screening for developmental handicaps in childhood	V79.3
Screening for congenital anomaly of eye	V80.2

Chapter 15—Certain Conditions Originating in the Perinatal Period (760-779)

It is easy to confuse this chapter with the previous chapter on congenital anomalies because both are concerned with conditions present during early childhood. The congenital anomaly chapter is descriptive of structural defects present at birth. The perinatal chapter includes some conditions that start in utero, but also others that occur as a result of the birth process or shortly thereafter. The perinatal period is defined as beginning before birth and lasting through the 28th day of life.

It could be possible to use one of these codes in an adult patient if there is no other code defining the condition for which the patient is being treated. Most conditions in this chapter do not last beyond infancy. However, some, such as bronchopulmonary dysplasia, can last for the lifetime of the patient and be the cause of later problems.

All clinically significant conditions noted on routine newborn examination should be coded. A condition is clinically significant if it requires clinical evaluation, therapeutic treatment, diagnostic procedures, extended hospital stay, increased nursing care or monitoring, or has implications for future health care needs.

Official coding guidelines for the perinatal chapter are:

Perinatal Conditions

Reason for Encounter	Use Code
Birth of infant	V30-39 categories
Care of infant transferred in after birth	Code(s) for condition(s) being treated (do not use V30-39)
Observation and evaluation of newborn or infant for suspected condition not found	V29 category
Infant being treated for health problem caused by maternal condition	760-763 categories
Prematurity or fetal growth retardation	Do not assign code based solely on weight or gestational age
Newborns testing HIV positive during the first 18 months of life	V01.79 unless physician documents symptomatic HIV infection

Other circumstances under which newborns are seen:

Reason for Encounter	Use Code
Need for prophylactic vaccinations	V03 to V06 categories

Chapter 16—Symptoms, Signs, and Ill-Defined Conditions (780-799)

At the beginning of Chapter 2 of this book, we defined a symptom as an observation you make about your body, a subjective opinion on your part. A sign is observable by the physician, an objective finding.

Since diagnosis sequencing is linked to payer reimbursement of health care providers, rules about sequencing signs and symptoms have been developed:

Reason for Encounter	Use Code
Treatment of a sign or symptom for which a definitive diagnosis is made	Code for definitive diagnosis
Treatment of a sign or symptom for which a definitive diagnosis has not yet been reached	Code for the sign or symptom
Treatment of a sign or symptom in an outpatient setting where no additional workup is performed	Code for the sign or symptom

The positioning of some conditions in Chapter 16 and other similar wordings in the individual disease chapters is sometimes puzzling. Abdominal pain is a symptom, while joint pain is considered a diagnosis. Male stress incontinence is a symptom, while female stress incontinence is a diagnosis.

This chapter also includes codes for nonspecific and nonspecific abnormal results of diagnostic tests. These codes would ordinarily not be used unless no additional information is available. They could, for example, be used as the reason for conducting additional testing to reach a clear diagnosis.

Chapter 17—Injury and Poisoning (800-999)

The last chapter in the ICD-9-CM Tabular List is huge. It covers not only what we ordinarily think of as injury and poisoning, but also burns and toxic effects of nonmedicinal substances. Significant levels of detail are required in physician documentation to assure correct coding of conditions from this chapter. Most of the code categories in this chapter have 5th digits to specify the precise anatomic site of injury.

Definitions of terms commonly used with injuries are helpful:

Fractures: a break, of any size, in a bone

- Closed: skin is intact
- Open: a break in the skin occurs (compound fracture)

In classifying skull fractures, the time period of any loss of consciousness should be known, along with the nature of any associated injuries.

Stress fractures are hairline cracks in bone that are due to repeated or prolonged force against the bone, not a blow to the bone. Sports or exercise can cause stress fractures. Because they are not considered an injury, they are found in the musculoskeletal chapter in ICD-9-CM (733.93-733.95), not the injury chapter.

Pathological fractures are caused by disease, not injury. The most common causes are osteoporosis and cancer. In these fractures, the bone structure itself is abnormal, contributing to the break. This group is also found in the musculoskeletal chapter (733.1X).

When a bone that forms part of a joint is displaced from that location, it is known as a dislocation. Dislocations can also be categorized as open if the skin is broken. A partial or incomplete dislocation is called a subluxation. These usually occur as a result of injury. In parallel with the classification of fractures, a dislocation due to disease rather than injury is found in the musculoskeletal chapter (718.2X).

Open Wounds

In addition to cuts, lacerations, and punctures, open wounds also include injuries such as animal bites (including human), traumatic amputation, and avulsion. The latter is defined as forcible pulling away of tissue.

- Complicated: an open wound is considered to be complicated if there is mention of delayed treatment, foreign body, delayed healing, or infection
- Uncomplicated: wounds without mention of complication

Superficial Injuries

These are grouped together in a separate category outside the standard classification. Included are:

- Abrasion or friction burns
- Blisters

- Insect bites
- Superficial foreign body (such as splinter)
- Other superficial injuries

This classification also divides further cases specifying infection and those with no mention of infection.

Foreign Bodies

Foreign bodies in open wounds are classified in that coding category. Superficial foreign bodies are classified with superficial injuries, as described immediately above. There is a separate category for the effects of foreign bodies entering through an orifice, or natural opening in the body. We are talking here about the pencil eraser in the ear, or the piece of steak stuck in the throat.

The official diagnosis coding guidelines related to injuries are:

Injuries and Fractures

Reason for Encounter	Use Code
Multiple injuries	Use separate code for each injury unless a combination code is available. Do not use multiple injury codes unless information for a specific code is not available
Multiple injuries	Sequence the code for the most serious injury first
Abrasions or contusions	Do not code if associated with more severe injuries of same site
Primary injury with minor damage to nerves or blood vessels	Sequence primary injury first
Multiple fractures of the same limb in same 3-digit or 4-digit category	Use combination category
Multiple fractures of same bones but different bone parts	Code individually by site
Multiple fractures	Sequence in order of severity
Dislocation associated with fracture of same site	Code fracture only

Burns

In addition to thermal burns due to flames, the ICD-9-CM burn classification includes burns caused by electricity, lightning, hot liquids (scalding), radiation, and hot objects.

In addition to coding the location or site of the burn, it is necessary to assign a second code to indicate the percentage of body area involved in the burn. This is calculated using what is known as the "rule of nines." Figure 2-5 illustrates the percentage of body surface associated with body areas:

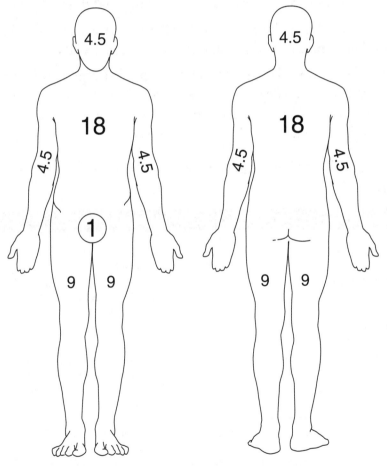

Figure 2-5   Rule of Nines

The "rule of palms" is useful for smaller areas. The size of the victim's palm is approximately 1% of body area, so the number of palms will equal the percentage. The definition for the smallest area code in ICD-9-CM is ten percent or less, so it is not necessary to measure precisely unless more than 10% is involved.

- First degree burn: only the outer layer of the skin, the epidermis, is involved. Symptoms include redness, tenderness, pain, and swelling.

- Second degree burn: penetrates into the dermis. The characteristics are: blisters, redness, swelling, and fluid seepage.

- Third degree burns: involves all three layers of the skin. The appearance of the skin is white, charred, and dry.

- ICD-9-CM also uses the term deep third degree, which is called fourth-degree in other references. These are third degree burns in which additional underlying structures such as bone, tendons, or joints are involved.

Official ICD-9-CM coding guidelines for burns are:

Burns

Reason for Encounter	Use Code
Multiple burns	Sequence the code for the highest degree of burn first
Multiple burns	Code separately. Only use the multiple burn code if location not documented
Non-healing burns, including necrosis of burned skin	Code as acute burns
Multiple burns of same local site but different degrees	Classify to sub-category of the highest degree recorded
Infected burn site	Use 953.8, posttraumatic wound infection
Mortality of burn victim during episode of care, or third degree burn of >20% body area	Use category 948. Fourth digit indicates total involvement. Fifth digit indicates % of third degree burns
Treatment of late effects of burns (scars, joint contractures)	Code for condition being treated plus code for late effect of burn

Poisoning, Adverse Effects and Toxicity

The definitions of these terms are a little different than those used in the average murder mystery:

- Poisoning occurs when a drug, medicinal substance, or other biological substance is not used correctly. This can occur through:
  - Wrong dosage taken by patient
  - Wrong dosage administered to patient
  - Medication taken by wrong person
  - Overdose (intentional or accidental)
  - Intoxication
  - Medications taken in combination with alcohol or over-the-counter medications
- Adverse effects occur when a drug is correctly prescribed and administered but there are side effects:
  - Drug allergy or hypersensitivity
  - Drug intoxication
  - Toxic effect of a drug
  - Drug toxicity (including cumulative effects)
- Toxic effects, from a coding perspective, refer to nonmedicinal substances such as chemicals, gases, metals, foods, and substances such as latex and silicone.

The ICD-9-CM coding manual includes a large table of drugs and chemicals that is used to locate the correct code for poisoning and the correct E-codes for external causes for each listed substance or drug.

The official diagnosis coding rules for these categories are:

Poisoning and Adverse Effects

Reason for Encounter	Use Code
Adverse effect of a drug correctly prescribed and properly administered	Code for adverse reaction plus E code for adverse effect
Condition caused by error in prescription or administration of drug	Code for poisoning plus code for manifestation
Intentional overdose	Code for poisoning plus code for manifestation
Nonprescribed drug in combination with correctly prescribed and administered drug	Code for poisoning plus code for manifestation
Toxic effect of nonmedicinal substances	Code for toxic effect (980–989) plus code to specify nature of toxic effect

Codes are also available for effects of other external causes:

- Environment: radiation, cold, heat and light, air pressure
- Child maltreatment syndromes
- Anaphylactic shock due to medications
- Anaphylactic shock due to food reactions
- Adult abuse and neglect
- Shock due to anesthesia

Complications of Surgical and Medical Care

Assignment of a code from this section does not imply that the surgical or medical care was inadequate. It does denote that a relationship between the previous care and the current condition has been documented, and that the current condition is more than routinely expected. There is no officially defined time limit on when the complication must occur.

Some complications are due to the presence of internal prosthetic devices, implants, and grafts. They may involve mechanical complications, such as breakage, leaking, obstructions, or they may involve infection or inflammatory reaction. Other complications such as pain, hemorrhage, stenosis, and fibrosis also have codes defined by the type of internal device.

Complications of organ transplants are also in this section, as are systemic conditions such as post-operative shock, accidental laceration during the procedure, post-op infections, blood transfusion reactions, foreign bodies accidentally left in the patient, and all of the other unfortunate circumstances that may occur.

Patients with conditions in the injury and poisoning chapter of ICD-9-CM may be seen for a variety of associated reasons:

Reason for Encounter	Use Code
Plastic surgery for cosmetic appearance	V50.1
Plastic surgery following healed injury	V51.8
Fitting and adjustment of prosthetic device or implant	V52.X
Fitting and adjustment of orthopedic devices; casts	V53.7
Aftercare involving removal of fracture plate or other internal fixation devices	V54.01
Aftercare for healing traumatic fracture	V54.1X
Physical therapy	V57.1
Occupational therapy	V57.21
Dressing change or suture removal	V58.3X
Aftercare following surgery for injury and trauma	V58.43
Surgery follow-up	V67.00
Follow-up following treatment of healed fracture	V67.4

Supplementary Classification of External Causes of Injury and Poisoning (E800-E999)

Known in coding lingo as the "E codes," this chapter provides a way to use additional codes to identify how and where an injury or poisoning happened. They are never used as the principal or first-listed code; they are always used in a supplementary fashion. They are used primarily for statistical purposes in gathering data on injury cause, extent, and location. This data can be used for injury prevention and education programs.

The major categories of E codes include transport accidents, falls, fire and flames, natural and environmental causes, assaults, self-inflicted injuries, and late effects.

E codes are not generally used in healthcare billing or reimbursement.

Supplementary Classification of Factors Influencing Health Status and Contact with Health Services (V01-V83)

This chapter in ICD-9-CM is used to identify situations in which patients who are not currently sick require health services. The tables previously displayed in describing the chapters of ICD-9-CM included V codes to be used for things like suture removal, routine exams, screening, and aftercare.

V codes are controversial in the healthcare reimbursement arena because they may represent services for which some payers will not pay. The official diagnosis coding guidelines have helped, in recent years, enforce appropriate coding and insurance coverage.

There are four primary circumstances for the use of V codes:

- When a person who is not currently sick encounters health services for a specific reason, such as to act as an organ donor, to receive prophylactic care such as inoculations or screenings, or to receive counseling on a health-related issue.

- When a person with a resolving disease or injury, or a chronic long-term condition requiring continuous care, encounters the health care system for specific aftercare of that disease or injury. Examples are dialysis for renal disease, chemotherapy for malignancy, and cast change. A diagnosis or symptoms code should be used instead of a V code whenever a current, acute diagnosis is being treated or a sign or symptom is being studied.

- When circumstances or problems influence a person's health status but are not in themselves a current illness or injury.

- For newborns, to indicate birth status.

V Code Category Definitions

Category	Definition
V01	**Contact / exposure:** Patients do not show any sign or symptom of a communicable disease but have been exposed to it. Used to indicate a reason for testing or as a secondary code to identify a potential risk
V03-V06	**Inoculations and vaccinations:** Patient is being seen for a prophylactic inoculation against a disease.
	Status codes: The patient is either a carrier of a disease or has the sequelae of a past disease or condition, which can include the presence of a prosthetic or mechanical device or transplanted organ from previous treatment.
V02	Carrier or suspected carrier of infectious disease
V08	Asymptomatic HIV infection status
V09	Infection with drug-resistant microorganisms
V21	Constitutional states in development, such as low birth weight
V22.2	Pregnant state, incidental
V26.5X	Sterilization status; patient has been sterilized
V42	Organ or tissue replaced by transplant
V43	Organ or tissue replaced by other means
V44	Artificial opening status (colostomy, tracheotomy, etc.)
V45	Other postsurgical states (pacemaker, bypass, etc.)
V46	Other dependence on machines (respiratory)
V49.6X	Upper limb amputation status
V49.7X	Lower limb amputation status
V49.81	Postmenopausal status
V49.82	Dental sealant status
V58.6X	Long-term current drug use (prescribed), such as anticoagulants, aspirin therapy, etc.
V83-84	Genetic carrier or susceptibility status
	History of codes: Indicate personal or family history
V10	Personal history of malignant neoplasm
V12-V13	Personal history of other diseases
V14	Personal history of allergy to medicinal agents

V Code Category Definitions (continued)

Category	Definition
V15	Personal history presenting hazards to health (other allergies, surgery, psychological trauma, abuse, tobacco use, etc.)
V16	Family history of malignant neoplasm
V17	Family history of chronic disabling disease (stroke, asthma, epilepsy, etc.)
V18-V19	Family history of other conditions (diabetes, kidney disease, congenital anomalies)
	Screening: Testing for disease or disease indicators in seemingly well individuals so that early detection and treatment can be provided. A V code is not used if the patient already has a sign or symptom.
V28	Antenatal screening
V73-V82	Special screening examinations
	Observation: Patient is being observed for a suspected condition that is ruled out.
V29	Observation and evaluation of newborns for suspected condition not found
V71	Observation and evaluation for suspected condition not found
	Aftercare: The initial treatment of a disease or injury has been performed and the patient requires continued care during the healing or recovery phase, or for the long-term consequences of the disease.
	V code is not used if the treatment is directed at a current condition. Exceptions are chemotherapy and radiation therapy.
V52	Fitting and adjustment of prosthetic device and implant
V53	Fitting and adjustment of other device
V54	Other orthopedic aftercare
V55	Attention to artificial openings (closure, cleaning)
V56	Encounter for dialysis
V57	Rehab procedures
V58.0	Radiotherapy
V58.11	Chemotherapy
V58.3X	Attention to surgical dressings and sutures
V58.41	Planned post-operative wound closure
V58.4X	Surgical aftercare
V58.81	Fitting and adjustment of catheters
V58.83	Therapeutic drug monitoring
V58.89	Other

Category	Definition
	Follow-up: Continuing surveillance following completed treatment of a disease, condition, or injury. The condition has been fully treated and no longer exists.
V24	Postpartum care and evaluation
V67	Follow-up examinations
V59	**Donor:** Living individuals who are donating blood or other body tissues to other. Not for self-donation or cadaveric donations.
	Counseling: Patient or family member receives assistance in the aftermath of an illness or injury for when support is required in coping with family or social problems.
V25	Contraceptive management
V26.33	Genetic counseling
V26.49	Procreative management
V61	Other family circumstances
V65.19	Consulting on behalf of another person
V65.3	Dietary surveillance and counseling
V65.4	Other
	Routine and administrative examinations: General check-up or exam such as pre-employment physical. Pre-op exam codes are for clearance only
V20.2	Well child check
V70.0	General medical exam
V72	Special investigations and exams
	Miscellaneous and nonspecific V codes:
V07	Need for isolation
V50	Elective surgery
V60-63	Housing, psychosocial issues
V64	Procedures not carried out
V66	Palliative (end of life) care
V68	Prescription renewals, death certificates, etc.
V58.2	Blood transfusion without diagnosis
V58.9	Unspecified aftercare
V69	Lifestyle problems
V72.5	Radiology exam without reason for test
V72.60	Lab test without reason

How Can You Code Your Conditions?

If you have a sign, symptom, or diagnosis that you want to code, follow these steps:

1. Look for the condition in the Alphabetical Index. You may have to look in more than one place. If you don't find it listed under one of the terms, look under the others.

2. Once you have found the term, look at everything indented beneath it to see if there are other words from your diagnosis statement that apply.

3. After you have located what seems to be the correct term in the alpha listing, look up the number in the Tabular List.

4. Make sure you read all of the notes associated with your numeric code. Some of the notes may be at the top of the heading under which your number is listed. Some of the notes are "includes" that tell you what is included under this number, while some are "excludes" that may point you to another chapter and diagnosis code.

Keeping Up To Date

ICD-9-CM is updated twice a year, effective October 1st and April 1st. Diagnosis and procedure codes are added to cover newly identified disease states and new techniques in surgery. CMS and the National Center for Health Statistics (NCHS) publish these agenda in the United States with the approval of the World Health Organization. The diagnosis section of ICD-9-CM is the responsibility of NCHS while CMS handles the procedure section. The other two Cooperating Parties on ICD-9-CM are the American Health Information Management Association (AHIMA) and the American Hospital Association (AHA). The Central Office on ICD-9-CM, housed at the American Hospital Association in Chicago, publishes *Coding*

Clinic, a quarterly publication covering updates, coding guidelines, and readers' questions.

It is imperative that you use the current version of ICD-9-CM to research or solve personal coding-related concerns. When codes are revised, the code used is based on the date of service of your procedure. There is no longer any grace period during which it is okay to use either old or new codes.

Misdiagnosis: The Wrong Path

The patient was a 39-year-old male previously in good health. He was on summer vacation near the ocean and over a two-day period participated in several strenuous activities, such as swimming, sailing, jogging, even putting out a small forest fire. He later experienced chills and was so tired that he went to bed early. By the next morning, one leg was weak. It became paralyzed by the afternoon, and in the evening the other leg was weakened. He had a temperature of 102 degrees Fahrenheit. The family physician who examined the patient decided he had a cold.

By the second day, the paralysis had spread to all body areas below the chest. A specialist examined the patient and decided the problem was a blood clot in the lower spinal cord. Not until the fifteenth day of the illness was another diagnosis made. The patient was Franklin Delano Roosevelt and the diagnosis was poliomyelitis.

Even after Roosevelt's death, the debate about the cause of his paralytic illness continues. At the time, the diagnosis of polio seemed appropriate because it was the most common cause of paralysis in the United States, it was contracted during the summer, and was accompanied by fever. Researchers looking at the diagnosis retrospectively point to the patient's age of 39 and the lack of physician knowledge about other potential causes as indicative of the fact that the actual culprit was Guillain-Barre syndrome, an autoimmune condition.[10]

Misdiagnosis can occur when:

- Doctors lack sufficient time to analyze thoroughly
- Testing is not performed in order to save money
- Knowledge about less common diseases is lacking
- Patients do not communicate complete information
- Tests are not completed due to patient noncompliance
- Testing errors occur (equipment failure, human error)
- Objective testing is not possible
- Diagnosis is difficult to confirm
- Diagnosis is required for desired treatment implementation (example is attention deficit hyperactivity disorder "ADHD" treated with methylphenidate)

If you obtain information that indicates to you that the wrong diagnosis has been made, it is important that you discuss the matter with your physician. He can review the facts with you and if necessary, change his opinion. It is important that the incorrect diagnosis does not remain on your medical record, as it could affect your future treatment and well-being.

References

[1]Documentation Guidelines—Evaluation and Management Services. Center for Medicare and Medicaid Services website. Available at: http://www.cms.gov/medlearn/emdoc.asp. Accessed September 4, 2004.

[2]ICD-9-CM Official Guidelines for Coding and Reporting. National Center for Health Statistics website. 2005. Available at: http://www.cdc.gov/nchs/data/icd9/icdguide.pdf. Accessed June 16, 2005.

[3]Department of Health and Human Services, Centers for Medicare and Medicaid Services, Transmittal B-01-61. September 26, 2001.

[4]*Federal Register*, Vol. 50, No. 147, July 31, 1985, pp. 31038–40.

[5]ICD-9-CM Official Guidelines for Coding and Reporting. National Center for Health Statistics website. 2003. Available at: http://www.cdc.gov/nchs/data/icd9/icdguide.pdf. Accessed September 7, 2004.

[6]American Psychiatric Association Task Force on DMS-IV. *Diagnostic and Statistical Manual of Mental Disorders, 4th ed.* Washington, DC: American Psychiatric Association; 1994.

[7]Department of Health and Human Services, Centers for Medicare and Medicaid Services, Transmittal AB-01-144. September 26, 2001.

[8]Beers M and Berkow R. *The Merck Manual of Diagnosis and Therapy.* Whitehouse Station, NJ: Merck Research Laboratories; 1999. Available at http://www.merck.com/mrkshared/mmanual/home.jsp. Accessed July 27, 2004.

[9]Brown F. *ICD-9-CM Coding Handbook With Answers.* Chicago: American Hospital Publishing; 2003.

[10]Goldman AS et al. What was the cause of Franklin Delano Roosevelt's paralytic illness? *Journal of Medical Biography.* 2003;11:232–240.

CHAPTER 3

Procedure Coding— Location, Location, Location

Coding Paths Diverge

In addition to the patient's diagnosis, the other pieces of information associated with every healthcare encounter are the procedure codes, the dates the procedures were performed, the location in which they were performed, and the physician or other provider who performed them.

The term "procedure coding" encompasses a wide variety of services to patients:

- Surgery: operative treatment of disease or injury
- Anesthesia: the process of blocking pain or other perceptions
- Radiology: the use of imaging modalities for diagnosis, interventional techniques, or radiation therapy for treatment
- Laboratory: testing performed on biological specimens to get information about the health of a patient

- Pathology: diagnosis of disease based on the gross and microscopic examination of cells and tissues
- Diagnostic testing: non-lab, non-radiologic testing to arrive at a diagnosis
- Evaluation and management: "visits" to evaluate patients and manage their care
- Psychiatric: treatment of mental or emotional disorders
- Osteopathic: branch of medicine that uses manipulative techniques to supplement treatment of disease
- Chiropractic: focuses on spinal function to improve health
- Rehabilitation: physical, occupational, speech, and other therapies to improve functioning
- Alternative: diagnostic or treatment methods with theoretical bases that differ from conventional medicine, such as acupuncture
- Preventive: actions, such as vaccinations, to prevent disease or injury

All types of providers, whether facilities or individual practitioners, use ICD-9-CM diagnosis codes (see Chapter 2). This is not true for procedure or supply codes. The type of billing code used depends on several factors:

- Location, or site of service where the procedure was performed
- Type of charge being coded:
  - Professional
  - Facility
  - Dental
  - Durable medical equipment, prosthetics, or supplies
  - Drugs and biologics

In this chapter, we will focus on procedure coding for professional services and facility services.

Hospital Procedures vs. Doctor's Procedures

As a case study, let's assume that you have always been in good health, but that over the past weekend, you started having pain in your stomach region. It started near your navel and then became more and more severe as it moved toward the lower right side of your abdomen. You decided to go to the emergency room. After the exam and some lab work, the doctor decided that you had appendicitis. A surgeon was contacted and you were taken to the operating room for an appendectomy, or removal of your appendix.

From the time you entered the emergency room to the time you were discharged home after recuperation from your surgery, the hospital maintained a medical record documenting every occurrence during your stay. In addition to documentation by the emergency room physician and the surgeon, your medical record also includes notes by the nursing staff, orders from physicians, reports of the results of diagnostic testing such as the lab work, administrative paperwork such as consent forms, visits by allied health personnel such as the dietitian, your vital signs, and details such as whether or not you went to the bathroom.

The surgeon who removed your appendix will also start a medical record for you at his office, even though you have not yet been there. At this point, it will probably contain a copy of the operative report dictated by the surgeon for the hospital record and a copy of the hospital "face sheet" of demographics with your name, address, and insurance information. When you visit the surgeon for a follow-up visit after your surgery, he will add a progress note to his office chart.

After you are discharged from the hospital, your medical record will be processed by the Health Information Department of that facility. It will be assembled into a standard order, checked for missing documentation and signatures, placed in a folder, and the diagnoses and procedures coded. In an increasing number of hospitals, all of the documentation is maintained electronically, lessening the need for, and reliance on, paper.

As a patient, you are issued a unique number under which all of your health information is maintained. These numbers are specific to a facility or chain of facilities only; they are not used across organizational boundaries, with a few exceptions. Known as a patient number, or medical record number, or patient identifier, this unique number follows you throughout your care. Patients who are admitted to the hospital as an inpatient generally receive a wristband with their name and medical record number. This is used to prevent identity errors and resulting incorrect medication administration, wrong surgery, or lab specimen errors.

Medical coding analysts will look at your record in order to assign ICD-9-CM diagnosis codes to your diagnosis "acute appendicitis," and they will also assign ICD-9-CM procedure codes to your procedure "appendectomy." They may also check the results of the surgical pathology examination of your appendix to determine whether or not you actually had appendicitis. The diagnosis code and procedure code will be routed to the hospital business office where a bill will be generated for the facility charges incurred during your stay. If you have insurance, a claim form with the diagnosis and procedure codes will be sent to that payer for reimbursement.

Meanwhile, the surgeon is also interested in getting paid. While the surgeon's claim form to your insurance company will usually contain the same ICD-9-CM diagnosis codes used by the hospital, the procedure code will be different. *Current Procedural Terminology*, also known as CPT, will be used by the surgeon.

Why the Difference? How Did It Come About?
Hospital Procedure Coding

Remember that coding started as a way to categorize deaths. It evolved into a method of indexing hospital diagnoses and procedures in order to assess the healthcare status and needs of the liv-

Figure 3-1   Florence Nightingale
Source: http://www.probert-encyclopedia.co.uk

ing. The first advocate of hospital statistics was Florence Nightingale, the famous nurse (Fig. 3-1).

While serving in a battlefront hospital during the Crimean War of the 1850s, she observed that far more soldiers died of disease than of war injuries. Her relentless efforts to improve sanitation reduced the mortality rate in her hospital from 40% to 2% in one year.[1] When she returned to England after the war, she submitted a statistical report to the British government, hoping to convince them that improvement of sanitary conditions in local hospitals would also reduce deaths. The government refused to allow her to publish her data. She persisted, using Army data already available, informing the public of her cause. When she began her campaign, life expectancy in England was 39 years. When she died 50 years later in 1910, it had risen to 55, at least in part due to her efforts.[2]

Before 1960, hospitals used various systems to index procedures. With the manual methods in use at that time, "indexing" literally meant using index cards. A card was set up for each procedure code or category, and the medical record numbers of patients who underwent that procedure were written on the card, along with the date of the procedure. At the same time, statistical reports were prepared showing how many of various procedures were performed monthly or annually. If researchers needed information on cases from a particular procedure category, the medical records could be pulled based on the information in the indexes.

The first revision of the International Classification of Diseases (ICD) that contained procedure codes was a version of ICDA-7 issued by the United States Public Health Service in 1959.[3] It contained procedure codes up to three digits. ICDA-8, also with three-digit codes, was used from 1970-78 and ICD-9-CM from 1979 to the present. The latter classification was expanded to 4-digit codes for procedures.

Concurrent with the development of consistent procedure coding systems was the initiation of the Uniform Hospital Discharge Data Set (UHDDS). Although vital statistics data, such as births, deaths, and marriages, had uniform definitions in the United States, there was no agreement before 1973 on what data should be collected and reported by hospitals. The National Center for Health Statistics collected hospital data, but the emphasis was on the institutions' overall activities, not the problems of their patients. The statistics described how busy they were, but not what they were accomplishing in the way of patient care.[4]

An amendment to the Public Health Act in 1974 made the National Committee on Vital and Health Statistics a statutory body and required that there be an annual report to Congress on the health of the American people. *Health United States 1975*[5] was a hit with the press (Fig. 3-2). It reported in one place, for the first time, 603 pages of health-related data, such as the average physician fee for an initial office visit ($12.17 for a pediatrician and $17.62 for a surgeon), and the average net income of physicians ($43,570 for a pediatrician and $62,320 for a surgeon).

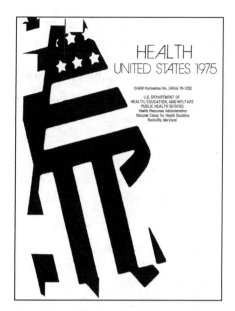

Figure 3-2   Health United States 1975

Hospital discharge data by diagnostic category was skimpy, and there was no information about hospital procedures except for the number of hospitals reporting various types of services, such as burn units, home care, renal dialysis, and blood banks.

Currently, the UHDDS Procedure Code Guidelines, developed in 1973 and revised in 1985, govern the types of procedure code data collected on hospital inpatients. Additional rules developed by Medicare with the advent of its Prospective Payment System (see Chapter 4) come into play because of the link between procedure coding and reimbursement.

Physician Procedure Coding

Prior to 1981, there were a number of different systems used to code physician procedures. There was no requirement that a code number be submitted with a claim for payment, so many physicians merely submitted a verbal description of what they had done. This required the insurance companies to figure out what some of the arcane descriptions meant before they could decide how much to pay.

When Medicare was enacted in 1965, physicians looked for a better system to report their services. What better group to design a physician coding system than their own professional organization, the American Medical Association (AMA)? The first edition of *Current Procedural Terminology* (CPT) was published by the AMA in 1966. Primarily containing surgical procedure codes, with smaller sections on medicine, laboratory, and radiology, it consisted of four-digit code numbers.

Expansion of CPT led to

- the adoption of 5-digit codes in CPT-2 (1970)
- the addition of modifiers for further specificity in reporting in CPT-3 (1973)
- the inclusion of additional codes for new technology in CPT-4 (1977).

In 1992, the Evaluation and Management (E&M) codes were added to describe cognitive efforts involved with non-surgical services. CPT is updated annually to reflect changes in medical and surgical services.

In 1983, the federal government entered into an agreement with the AMA that CPT would be the mechanism for reporting physician services under Medicare. As is usually the case, other payers follow Medicare procedures and by 1990 CPT had become the single uniform system for reporting of physician services. Today it is estimated that over 95% of services provided by physicians are reported using the CPT coding system.[6]

While ICD-9-CM is a system in the public domain, CPT remains a proprietary system owned and operated by the AMA. It is not possible to obtain a copy of CPT without purchase.

What about HCPCS?

This system (pronounced hick-picks) is the Healthcare Common Procedure Coding system. CPT is part of HCPCS, known as Level I. There are also more than 4,000[7] alpha-numeric Level II codes, used to identify health care equipment and supplies and drugs. The descriptors of Level II codes identify like items or services, rather than specific brand names. For example, HCPCS code J3410 has the description of "Hydroxyzine HCl up to 25mg." This code does not vary, even if the drug administered is a brand name formulation rather than generic. The same code is used regardless of manufacturer or supplier. If you visit your doctor and he administers a medication to you during the visit, his claim form to the payer will include a CPT code for his service plus a HCPCS Level II J code for the medication. Retail pharmacies use yet another coding system, the National Drug Codes (NDC). Under consideration is the elimination of the HCPCS J codes and the requirement that all providers and suppliers use the NDC codes. The NDC codes are eleven digits long, which is problematic for the billing systems in many doctors' offices.

Dental codes, *Current Dental Terminology* (CDT), are also part of HCPCS Level II. CDT is maintained by the American Dental Association and is used only for dental billing.

"Miscellaneous" and "temporary" HCPCS Level II codes change frequently, and are used for brand new items or services that haven't yet made it to the permanent section of codes. Miscellaneous codes can be used to bill for items for which no other codes exist.

The fact that CPT is part of HCPCS, and the existence of the 1983 agreement that the AMA would have the "sole responsibility and authority to revise, update, or modify" CPT and to "continue to print, publish, sell, and otherwise disseminate"[8] CPT even though it is being used as part of a required code set for federal health program billing purposes, has caused accusations that the government "granted the AMA what has been characterized as a 'statutory monopoly' . . . a financial windfall for the AMA in the form of CPT-related book sales and royalties approaching $71 million a year."[9]

The Health Insurance Portability and Accountability Act (HIPAA) of 1996 requires, under its Administrative Simplification section, that the Department of Health and Human Services define national standards for the electronic transaction of health care information, including provider and facility claims. As of October 16, 2003, standard code sets had to be implemented by all parties who transmit information electronically. ICD-9-CM is the standard code set for diagnoses, while ICD-9-CM procedure codes are the rule for inpatient hospital procedures, CDT for dental services, and HCPCS (including the AMA-controlled CPT) for:

- physician services
- physical and occupational therapy services
- radiological procedures
- clinical laboratory tests
- other medical diagnostic procedures
- hearing and vision services
- transportation services, including ambulance

The designation of CPT as a standard code set under HIPAA further reinforced its position as the major procedure coding authority.

Where It's At

The location where the service or product is provided determines which code set is used. As is the case with many other facets of healthcare billing, the methods of identifying the location differ between professional claims and facility claims. Professional billing uses Place of Service codes defined by the Centers for Medicare and Medicaid Services (CMS). Facility billing uses the concept of "bill type," a three digit numeric code where the first digit represents the type of facility, the second digit represents the classification, and the third digit equals the frequency of the bill.[10] The following table shows the correlation between common types of the two location designations:

Facility Bill Type	Description	Professional Location
11X 12X	Hospital inpatient	21 (inpatient hospital) 51 (psychiatric)
13X	Hospital outpatient	22 (outpatient hospital) 23 (hospital emergency room)
14X	Hospital other	20 (urgent care)
21X	Skilled nursing	31 (skilled nursing facility)
33X	Home health	12 (patient home)
71X	Rural health clinic	72 (rural health clinic)
72X	Freestanding dialysis center	65 (end-stage renal disease facility)
74X	Outpatient rehab	
75X	Comprehensive outpatient rehab	62 (comprehensive outpatient rehab facility)
76X	Community mental health center	53 (community mental health center)
83X	Hospital outpatient ASC (ambulatory surgical center)	24 (ambulatory surgical center)

There are a number of additional professional services place of service or location codes for places where a facility would not be submitting a bill to a federal payer. These include:

03 School

04 Homeless shelter

11 Doctor's office

13 Assisted living facility

14 Group home

26 Military treatment facility

32 Nursing facility

33 Custodial care facility

55 Residential substance abuse treatment facility

56 Psychiatric residential treatment center

The location or place of service is important in coding because many payers have different reimbursement schedules, co-pay amounts, or coverage limitations depending on where the service is provided.

The Evaluation and Management (E&M) codes in CPT are defined based on location:

- Hospital inpatient
- Office or other outpatient
- Hospital observation
- Emergency department
- Nursing facility (skilled, intermediate, long term care, psychiatric, residential treatment center)
- Boarding home or custodial care
- Home (private residence)

ICD-9-CM Procedure Coding Guidelines
(Hospital Inpatients Only)

Item 12 of the UHDDS guidelines[11] states that procedure codes and dates of all significant procedures are to be reported. The identity (number) of the person performing the procedure must also be reported.

What is a "significant procedure"? One or more of the following:

- Surgical in nature
  - Incision
  - Excision
  - Amputation
  - Introduction
  - Endoscopy
  - Repair
  - Destruction
  - Suture
  - Manipulation
- Carries a procedural risk
  - Professionally recognized risk that a procedure may potentially cause body impairment, injury, disease, or death
  - Trauma risk—procedures that are invasive, able to produce tissue damage, or introduce toxic or noxious substances
  - Physiologic risk—procedures that use any drug or physical substance that can affect the body
  - Any procedure using pre- or post-operative medications
  - Procedures that use long-life radioisotopes

- Carries an anesthestic risk
  - Any procedure using general anesthesia
  - Any local, regional, or other type of anesthesia causing functional impairment that requires care in usage to protect the patient from harm
- Requires specialized training
  - Specialized professionals, qualified technicians, or clinical teams specifically trained for the performance of the procedure

Principal Procedure

The principal procedure is one that was performed for definitive treatment rather than one performed for diagnostic or exploratory purposes, or was necessary to take care of a complication. If two procedures appear to meet this definition, then the one most related to the principal diagnosis should be selected as the principal procedure.

Selection of the principal procedure is related to inpatient reimbursement (see Chapter 4). Because there is the potential of manipulating coding in order to receive a higher reimbursement rate, coding guidelines for the selection of principal diagnosis and sequencing of other procedures were developed.

The selection of the principal procedure is not always clear-cut. Let's go back to our case sample in which you were admitted as an inpatient and had an appendectomy to resolve your appendicitis. If, during your hospital stay, you fell out of bed and broke your hip, you might have undergone an additional surgery to repair your hip fracture. Both the appendectomy and the hip surgery meet the criteria of being performed for definitive treatment. Even though the hip repair is a more expensive procedure taking more time, the appendectomy is the principal diagnosis because it is most related to your principal diagnosis of appendicitis.

If more than one procedure is equally related to the principal diagnosis, the most resource-intensive or complex procedure is generally designated as the principal procedure.

Other Procedure Coding Guidelines

Diagnostic endoscopy with biopsy: the endoscopy procedure involves a higher degree of skill and has greater risk. The endoscopy is sequenced first, with the biopsy second. Biopsies performed via endoscopy or percutaneous needle aspiration are closed biopsies. Incision for removal of tissue for biopsy purposes is an open biopsy.

Biopsy with inadvertent removal: Only the intended biopsy. Inadvertent biopsies are not considered complications of procedures.

Excisional biopsy: When the entire lesion is removed, excision of lesion should be coded. When only part of the lesion is removed, a biopsy is coded.

Definitive surgery is defined as:

- Surgery that restores or repairs
- Surgery that removes diseased body parts
- Surgery that removes foreign material
- Surgery to assist obstetrical delivery

Exploratory surgery: when followed by definitive surgery, is coded only to the definitive surgery performed. There are two exceptions to this rule:

- Exploratory surgery followed by biopsy; code both procedures
- Exploratory surgery followed by incidental appendectomy; code both procedures

<u>Aborted or incomplete procedures:</u> code the procedure to the extent that it was carried out.

<u>Cancelled procedures:</u> Do not code any procedure. Use a diagnosis code from category V64 to indicate that the procedure for this episode of care was cancelled.

<u>"Failed" procedures:</u> If a procedure did not accomplish every objective or failed to achieve the expected result, it is still coded as performed. Procedure coding is the classification of work performed, not the outcome.

<u>Bilateral procedures:</u> If no separate code exists to identify a procedure as bilateral, code it twice.

<u>Endoscopic procedures:</u> If no code is available for an endoscopic, laparoscopic, or thoracoscopic procedure, the open procedure code is used. If a laparoscopic procedure is converted to an open procedure, only the open procedure is coded, but an additional diagnosis code, V64.4, is used to indicate this circumstance.

If a biopsy is performed endoscopically and no code exists for the endoscopic performance of the biopsy, the biopsy is coded and the endoscopy is also coded.

How to Locate a Procedure

The method for finding a procedure in ICD-9-CM is the same as that for ICD-9-CM diagnosis coding. There is an alphabetical index and a tabular list for verification. Many procedures are eponymic, named after the surgeon who developed the procedure. If no entry in the alphabetical index is found under the eponymic name for the operation, it is necessary to read the operative report to identify the type of procedure and then search the index for the procedure with the technique or methods most closely approximating the eponymic procedure. A list of the two-digit procedure coding categories found in ICD-9-CM is contained in Appendix B of this book.

CPT Procedure Coding (All Medical and Surgical Services Other Than Hospital Inpatient)

CPT (Current Procedural Terminology) codes consist of 5 numbers representing a unique service. The classification structure is divided into six main sections:

- Anesthesia   (00100 to 01999)
- Surgery   (10040 to 69990)
- Radiology   (70010 to 79999)
- Pathology and Laboratory   (80048 to 89399)
- Medicine   (90281 to 99199)
- Evaluation and Management   (99201 to 99499)

Despite the fact that the system is divided into categories, a CPT code from any category may be used by any physician or surgeon, regardless of specialty. The Evaluation and Management section is used by all specialties and represents some of the most frequently billed services. Code 99213, which is an office visit for an established patient, was the number one procedure code submitted to Medicare in 2002, with more than 105 million visits totaling more than $5 billion in allowed charges.[12]

The index to CPT is organized alphabetically and includes main terms that may denote a procedure or service, an organ or anatomic site, a condition, or synonyms, eponyms or abbreviations. When searching the index, if a listing is not found under what appears to be the main term, search under one of the other words in the procedure description. Once a main term has been located, review the subterms below it to determine which is the most appropriate given the description of the procedure that was performed.

Unlike ICD-9-CM procedure coding, there are no official national rules governing the use of CPT. However, CPT codes can also be a determinant in reimbursement, so various governmental agencies have developed their own guidelines to assure consistency and conformity to coding definitions. Each section of CPT itself also has instructions applicable to that section.

If the CPT definition of a code includes a defined time period, there must be documentation from the physician indicating how much time they spent performing the service. An example of this would be 90804, which is "Individual psychotherapy, insight oriented, behavior modifying and/or supportive, in an office or outpatient facility, approximately 20 to 30 minutes face-to-face with the patient." Codes with the time specified in the definition are known as "time-based" codes.

Sometimes there is no existing CPT code that adequately describes the procedure performed. This may be due to new techniques, additional technological developments, or procedures performed on anomalous anatomy caused by congenital malformations. Each section of CPT has an "unlisted" code, usually ending in "99" that is to be used in this situation. It is important to note that the presence of a code in CPT describing a service does not mean that a specific third-party payer will reimburse for that service (see Chapter 4).

CPT Modifiers

An additional feature of CPT is the use of "modifiers" to indicate that specific circumstances have changed the performed service. An example would be the use of modifier -50 to indicate that a procedure not already defined as bilateral was performed on both sides of the body at the same episode of care. Modifiers play a key role in explaining to payers why procedures that look like they should not be paid separately are in fact justified.

Some of the most commonly used HCPCS modifiers are:[13]

- -22 Unusual procedural service. Service greater than that usually required. This could occur if, for example, a surgeon is operating on a patient who is grossly obese. It takes more work to cut through additional tissue.

- -24 Unrelated E&M service by the same physician during a post-operative period. If you fall and break your ankle and have surgical repair, there is a 90-day global period after the surgery where follow-ups are included in the charge for the surgery. If you fall and break your wrist during that time and go to the same doctor, he would use a -24 modifier on your office visit to tell the payer it is unrelated to the previous surgery.

- -25 This modifier indicates that two procedures were performed during the same episode of care. One was an evaluation and management (E&M) service such as an office visit, and the other was a procedure. Normally, the visit would be included in the charge for the procedure but if there is significant separate documentation of the E&M, using both procedure codes could be justified. This situation often occurs when a patient comes in for an office visit for ongoing medical conditions, such as hypertension, and if they have another problem that requires a procedure, such as removing a wart.

- -26 Professional component of a service. Many procedures have a professional component and a technical component. An example is a chest x-ray. The technical component consists of the equipment used to do the x-ray, the salary of technician who performs the exam, and the costs of supplies such as films. The professional component is for the physician who interprets the films and documents his findings.

- -27 This modifier may be used by hospitals to tell the payer that the patient had multiple E&M encounters on the same date. This could occur if a patient returns due to a problem, or if a patient is seen by different providers, such as specialist consultants, on the same day. The modifier would be used on the second and subsequent E&M code.

- -50 Modifier -50 indicates a procedure was performed bilaterally. It can only be used for procedures that can anatomically be bilateral. For example, a bladder procedure could not be bilateral because you only have one bladder. Some CPT codes already indicate that the procedure is bilateral, such as 58605 Ligation or transection, fallopian tube(s). This code would be used for all operations of this type, whether unilateral or bilateral. It would not be appropriate to add a -50 modifier to this code for a bilateral procedure.

- -51 Multiple procedures. When multiple surgeries are performed at the same operative session, modifier -51 may be used on the second, third, fourth, etc. procedure codes to indicate multiple procedures. Many payers reduce their reimbursement percentage on the second, third, etc. procedures, only paying 100% of their fee schedule for the first procedure.

- -52 On some occasions, a service may be partially reduced or eliminated at the discretion of the physician. This could include a time-based procedure that is not performed for the entire time specified in the code description.

- -53 Surgical procedure terminated after the start of anesthesia, due to extenuating circumstances, for the well-being of the patient. This modifier is used only for physician professional services; it is not used for hospital facility outpatient billing.

- -57 Decision for surgery. This modifier can be used by, for example, the surgeon who performed your appendectomy, in order to bill for the visit on which he decided that you needed surgery. If the visit and the surgery occur on the same calendar date, the payer would normally consider the visit to be part of the surgical package. Using the modifier -57 tells the payer that the surgeon did not make the decision to do surgery until that day. Obviously this modifier cannot be used with elective, scheduled procedures.

- -58 Staged or related procedure during the post-operative period. This would be to denote a procedure that was planned at the time of the original procedure, more extensive than the original procedure, or a therapeutic procedure following a diagnostic surgical procedure. If the second procedure is for a complication of the first, and a return trip to the operating room is required, then a modifier -78 is used instead.

- -59 This modifier can be used to indicate that a procedure was distinct or separate from other procedures performed on the same date. Let's assume that you had two skin lesions, one on each arm, that are excised by a dermatologist. Since the skin is considered to be a single organ covering the entire body, these cannot be coded as bilateral procedures. It would be appropriate to code the first excision and then code the second with a -59 modifier to indicate the separate site. This tells the insurance company that the doctor is not inadvertently submitting a duplicate procedure. The -59 can be used for a different site, separate lesion or injury, a different operative session, or patient encounter.

- -62 Co-surgeons jointly performing a single procedure. Each surgeon bills the same code with a -62 modifier. Payment to each is usually 62.5% of the normal amount.

- -73 Discontinued outpatient hospital or ambulatory surgery center (ASC) procedure prior to the administration of anesthesia. This modifier is used by hospitals or ASCs to demonstrate use of their resources when the patient is prepared for surgery and taken to the room where the procedure is to be performed, but the procedure is canceled before anesthesia has been administered. This could happen if the patient's blood pressure is too high, if new lab results reveal contra-indications to surgery, or other reasons. If a procedure is cancelled before the patient goes to the procedure room, the procedure is not reported at all.

- -74 Modifier -74 is the hospital outpatient equivalent of modifier -53 used by physicians. It identifies procedures that are discontinued after the administration of anesthesia. If more than one procedure was planned, and one or more completed, the completed procedure(s) would be reported without the modifier. It should only be used if none of the procedures was fully completed.

- -76 Repeat procedure by same physician. Same exact procedure, same site, same doctor, same date. This modifier is often used with radiological procedures performed more than once on a date, as required by the patient's condition. Another example would be multiple EKGs to monitor a patient's heart condition.

- -77 Repeat procedure by another physician. Same procedure, same site, same date, different doctor. Just like modifier -76, but a different physician performed the second or subsequent procedure.

- -78 Return to the operating room for a related procedure during the post-operative period. This modifier is often used when complications of the original procedure require an additional procedure.

- -79 Unrelated procedure or service by the same physician during the post-operative period. This is the surgical equivalent of modifier -24.

- -80 Assistant surgeon. This doctor bills the same code as the surgeon but adds an -80 modifier.

- -91 Repeat clinical lab. Used when multiple results are necessary in the course of treatment on the same date. Should not be used for repeats due to equipment failure or inadequate specimens. If the second test is performed on a specimen from a different site, modifier -59 should be used instead of modifier -91.

In addition to the modifiers listed previously, there are anesthesia modifiers identifying the type of provider and supervision, other anatomical modifiers for fingers, toes, eyelids, coronary arteries, and situational modifiers for ambulance services, mammography, durable medical equipment (DME), and orthotics and prosthetics. Different payers may have different rules about which modifiers are valid in various service locations.

Additional CPT Coding Guidelines

Each section of CPT has coding guidelines to direct the use of the codes in that section:

Anesthesia

The services in this section include pre- and post-operative visits, anesthesia care during the procedure, fluid or blood administration, and standard monitoring of vital signs, heart rate and rhythm. In addition, there is an official definition of "anesthesia time," which "begins when the anesthesiologist begins to prepare the patient for the induction of anesthesia in the operating room or an equivalent area and ends when . . . the patient may be safely placed under post-operative supervision."[14]

Each anesthesia case also has an indicator of how sick the patient was. Some payers will increase the amount of reimbursement for sicker patients:

P1 = Normal healthy patient

P2 = Patient with mild system disease

P3 = Patient with severe systemic disease

P4 = Patient with severe systemic disease that is a constant threat to life

P5 = Moribund patient who is not expected to survive without the operation

P6 = Brain-dead patient whose organs are being removed for donor purposes[15]

Separate codes are also available to denote patients under age 1 or over age 70, emergency anesthesia, and the use of total body hypothermia or controlled hypotension.

Surgery

Codes in this section always include the following services in what is known as a "surgical package." This means that these services should not be billed in addition to the code for the surgical procedure:

- local infiltration, metacarpal/metatarsal/digital block, or topical anesthesia
- one related evaluation and management encounter on the day before or the day of surgery (apart from the decision for surgery)
- immediate post-operative care, such as talking with the patient's family, dictating the operative report
- writing orders
- evaluating the patient in the postanesthesia recovery unit
- typical post-op follow-up care[16]

The timeframe for the surgical package, or global period, is related to the seriousness of the surgery and the length of time needed for follow-up. The standard periods are:

- 0 days: day of surgery only
- 10 days: day of surgery and 10 days after (11 days total)
- 90 days: day before surgery, day of surgery and 90 days after (92 days total)

Care for complications or unrelated problems is not included and could be billed separately during the global period using the modifiers defined above to indicate the situation.

Surgical coding is based on the documentation in your medical record. For procedures that are performed in an operating room, the surgeon writes or dictates an operative report in which he describes the procedures performed, the type of anesthesia used, the techniques employed, specimens removed, estimated blood loss, preoperative and post-operative diagnoses, the names of the surgeon and any assistants, and whether or not any complications occurred.

Some of the procedure categories in the surgery section are coded using methods requiring precise measurements. For example, skin lesion removal is categorized according to the method of removal, whether or not the lesion is benign or malignant (cancerous), and the size of the lesion. In the case of cancerous lesions, the margin of surrounding skin that is removed is also counted. If the physician does not document all of this, the coder has to rely on the measurements in the pathology report, which may be smaller due to shrinkage of the specimen. Suturing of wound repairs also relies on size. In this type of coding, the lengths of wounds repaired in the same manner in the same anatomical group are added together to get the final measurement and code.

In the musculoskeletal category, one must be mindful of the fact that fracture treatment (open or closed) can be confused with the type of fracture (open or closed). It is possible to perform an open treatment of a closed fracture. Open treatment refers to surgical opening of the fracture site; internal fixation devices may be used to treat the fracture.

Many procedures are now performed endoscopically. A surgical endoscopy always includes a diagnostic endoscopy. It may be appropriate to use more than one code for an endoscopy if more than one procedure is performed at the same session, such as removal of foreign body, biopsy, snare, dilation, control of bleeding.

An oft-used category in the surgery section is Maternity Care and Delivery. Obstetrics has a global package of services just like surgery. It is defined as:

- Antepartum care: monthly visits up to 28 weeks, biweekly visits to 36 weeks, and weekly visits until delivery

- Delivery: admission to the hospital, management of uncomplicated labor, vaginal or cesarean delivery

- Postpartum care: hospital and office visits following delivery

Radiology

Some radiologic procedures are coded using what is known as "component coding." This occurs when part of the procedure is actually a surgical procedure, while the other part is the radiological supervision and interpretation. An example is a knee arthrogram, which is an x-ray study of the knee joint after the injection of contrast media which makes the details of the joint more visible. In this case there is one code for the injection and a second code for the radiological supervision and interpretation of the films. If the radiologist does both procedures, he gets to bill both. If an orthopedist does the injection, then the radiologist only bills for the supervision and interpretation. The separate code for injection of contrast is not used if the code description for a CT, MRA, or MRI defines a procedure as being "with contrast." An example is 73701, defined as "computed tomography, lower extremity, with contrast material."

Component coding is also used in interventional radiology, in which catheters may be threaded through blood vessels to treat conditions located far from the point of entry. An example would be inserting a catheter into an artery in the leg and maneuvering it through the body to the location of an aneurysm (weak spot in the wall of a blood vessel), possibly in the brain. A detachable coil is passed through the catheter and left at the aneurysm site. The body reacts to the coil by forming a blood clot around it, thus strengthening the wall of the blood vessel. Interventional radiology coding requires extensive knowledge of anatomy as well as thorough documentation by the radiologist of the entry site, all vessels imaged, and any contrast injections performed.

Radiation oncology and radiopharmaceutical therapy are also part of this section. They include codes for various types of radiation or radiopharmacy therapy for cancer. In addition to the actual treatments themselves, there are codes for clinical treatment planning, which involves localization of the tumor, measurement of the patient's body contour, and calculation of the optimum treatment sequences to treat the diseased area while protecting other organs from adverse effects of radiation.

Mammography is a frequently performed radiologic procedure. Screening mammograms are performed on a regular basis as a preventive measure in the identification of breast cancer. If a patient has abnormal findings, a diagnostic mammogram may be done.

Pathology and Laboratory

This section is challenging to coding analysts because of the variety of personnel involved in laboratory testing and because of the use of "panels" to lump certain groups of tests together. Some laboratory procedures are performed by physicians while others are performed by technicians under the supervision of a physician.

Surgical pathology involves the gross and microscopic exam of different types of tissue that were removed at surgery. The gross exam is the appearance of the specimen to the eyes of the pathologist, while the microscopic exam is the examination of portions of the tissue specimen under a microscope. An autopsy is similar to surgical pathology except that it is the examination of the body after death. It is performed to determine the cause of death or to verify the diagnosis.

Medicine

Services in this section are primarily diagnostic procedures from a variety of specialties, including some that would normally be thought of as surgical, not medical, such as ophthalmology (eye) and otorhinolaryngology (ear, nose, and throat). Psychiatry is one of the specialties covered in this section. Many of the codes in the psychiatry section are time-based codes.

CPT also contains a few codes for services thought of as alternative therapies, such as acupuncture. Practitioners who use alternative treatments have initiated their own code set, known as "Alternative Billing Codes (ABC)" codes, which are authorized under HIPAA as acceptable for internal, statistical, and cash transactions, but are not yet part of the official code set recognized under HIPAA for third-party billing.[17]

Evaluation and Management

Last in numerical order, but certainly not last in terms of utilization for billing purposes, the evaluation and management section is probably the least understood and most controversial. Prior to 1992, this section occupied only four pages in CPT. The coding system for office visits was simple, based on four levels of visits.

The year 1991 was busy in the healthcare coding world. The predecessor of the Centers for Medicare and Medicaid Services (CMS), the Health Care Financing Administration (HCFA), implemented a new fee schedule for Medicare services. It was based on a system known as RBRVS, or the Resource-Based Relative Value Scale system. The system assigned relative value units to each CPT code, based on physician work effort, practice expense, and malpractice insurance expense. The system was an effort to move away from the previous "usual and customary" method of calculating fees based on prevailing charges that was faulted for driving up the cost of health care.

The RBRVS also recognized that the cognitive efforts expended by primary care providers such as internists, family practitioners, and pediatricians needed to be more highly valued in comparison to surgical services. A new scheme for coding office visits and other E&M services was implemented in 1992. The instructions and guidelines for these services now occupy 44 pages in CPT, compared with 4 pages prior to 1991.[18] The medical profession was not happy with these new codes because they required substantial amounts of additional documentation. Many practitioners felt they had to document items that were not essential to patient care in order to justify their billing.

There are currently two sets of documentation guidelines issued by Medicare: 1995 and 1997. Physicians may use either criteria set. A draft revision of the guidelines was released in 2000, and CMS contracted with a private firm to develop clinical vignettes to provide guidance on coding for various medical specialties. The 2000 guidelines were never implemented. In fact, a federal Health and Human Services Advisory Committee on Regulatory Reform voted in 2002 to abolish the E&M guidelines.

Put bluntly, physicians do not like these codes. They are extremely complex and difficult to interpret. In studies where physicians and coding analysts assigned E&M codes to hypothetical cases, the coding analysts agreed with expert opinion only 57%[19] of the time, while the agreement by physicians was only 52%.[20] This indicates a lot of gray areas in coding these services.

In Chapter 2 of this book, you learned about the three key components of an evaluation and management service: history, exam, and medical decision-making. It is these components that the physician must tally when arriving at an overall level for the E&M service. For example, a level four established patient office visit, for which Medicare will reimburse about $75 in Oklahoma ($100 in New York City) requires a detailed history, a detailed exam, and moderately complex decision-making. To document this level and justify this claim to your payer, your doctor will have to document:

- at least 4 elements of the history of present illness
- 2 to 9 systems reviewed
- 1 part of the past / family / or social history
- 5 to 7 body areas or systems examined

- 3 types of data reviewed
- existing problems that are worsening, or new problems that may or may not require additional workup
- risks of treatment options or procedures proposed

The AMA has defined the average amount of time for this level of visit as 25 minutes. If your doctor spends 25 minutes with you and more than half of that time is spent on counseling and coordination of care, such as talking with you about test results, treatment options, prognosis and risk factors, the doctor can bill for a level four visit without documenting all of the key component items listed above. He merely has to state "I spent more than 50% of this 25-minute visit discussing _____ with the patient."

If we assume that the physician works a 10-hour day, with an hour for lunch, he has a total of 540 minutes to see patients. He can accommodate 21 patients at 25 minutes apiece if he bills based on the amount of time he spends talking with you. Or, he can adopt methods that allow him to document all of the required pieces quicker in order to get the same level of payment in fewer minutes. Using the latter approach, he could conceivably double the number of patients seen, thus doubling his reimbursement. This is legitimate, assuming that all the necessary documentation is present in your medical record. An argument could be made that the E&M system rewards documentation and not face-to-face patient care.

The process for assigning an evaluation and management code is:

- Determine the location (place of service) where the E&M service was performed.
- Select the appropriate category of E&M code based on the location.

- Score the documentation counting the elements of the key components (history, exam, medical decision-making) or using the counseling and coordination of care option.

Under normal circumstances, a physician may only bill one evaluation and management service per day. If your doctor sees you in his office and decides that you are so sick you need to be admitted to the hospital, then stops by the hospital later that day to see you, he must "roll up" the office services into the code for the initial inpatient hospital care. Likewise, if you go to the emergency room and the ER physician decides you need to be observed for a period of time to monitor your condition, he may place you in observation status. The emergency room service must be "rolled up" into the observation service code for that date. Exceptions to the rule of one E&M per day would need to be justified through the use of modifiers indicating the circumstance.

Critical care in CPT terms does not occur just because you are in a critical care unit. Sometimes patients in those units may be there because they are awaiting a bed elsewhere in the hospital, awaiting the completion of discharge or transfer arrangements, or other administrative reasons. In order to meet the CPT definition of critical care, the patient must be critically ill or injured, to the extent that one or more vital organ system is impaired and there is a high probability of imminent or life-threatening deterioration in the patient's condition. In addition, the service provided must involve highly complex medical decision-making to assess, manipulate, and support single or multiple vital organ system failure or prevent further life-threatening deterioration of the patient's condition.[14]

CPT codes for adult critical care are time-based: for the first 30 minutes (or less), and then for each additional 30 minutes. The physician must clearly document their time spent. For children 24 months of age or less, the critical care codes are "per day" codes which means that all critical care services that date are included.

Procedure Coding Summarized

In this chapter, you have learned that procedure coding depends on the location where the service is provided and the type of charge being coded.

	Hospital Inpatients	**All Others**
Facility Bill	ICD-9-CM procedure codes	CPT / HCPCS procedure codes
Physician Bill	CPT / HCPCS procedure codes	CPT / HCPCS procedure codes

Procedure coding also depends, ultimately, on the physician's documentation in your medical record. The physician may know that he performed a procedure, but if it isn't documented, it wasn't done, as far as the coder is concerned.

Up to the Minute

As mentioned in Chapter 2 of this book, ICD-9-CM is updated twice annually. The CPT Editorial Panel, in conjunction with medical and surgical specialty societies, receives and reviews suggestions for changes to CPT; it is updated annually, effective on January 1st. When codes change, the date of service of the procedure determines whether an old or new code is appropriate. It is imperative that the current version of CPT be used for coding and payment purposes.

References

[1] The Passionate Statistician. Florence Nightingale Museum Trust, London. Available at http://www.florence-nightingale.co.uk. Accessed September 25, 2004.

[2] Small H. *Florence Nightingale, Avenging Angel.* New York: St. Martin's Press; 1998.

[3] United States Public Health Service. *International Classification of Diseases, Adapted for Indexing Hospital Records by Diseases and Operations.* Publication No. 719. Washington: U.S. Dept. of Health, Education, and Welfare, Public Health Service, National Center for Health Statistics; 1959.

[4] White K. *Reflections on the Past and Challenges for the Future.* The U.S. National Committee on Vital and Health Statistics. Available at http://www.ncvhs.hhs.gov/ncvhs50white.htm. Accessed September 25, 2004.

[5]United States Department of Health, Education, and Welfare. Public Health Service. Health Resources Administration. National Center for Health Statistics. *Health United States 1975.* Available at http://www.cdc.gov/nchs/hus/husacc75.pdf. Accessed September 25, 2004.

[6]Harris T. *Physician's Current Procedural Terminology (CPT).* Statement of the American Medical Association to the Subcommittee on Health Data Needs, Standards and Security, National Committee on Vital Health Statistics Department of Health and Human Services, April 16, 1997. Available at http://www.aapsonline.org/medicare/amacpt.htm. Accessed September 25, 2004.

[7]Medicare Program: Procedures for Coding and Payment Determinations for Clinical Laboratory Tests and for Durable Medical Equipment, 7/16/04. Centers for Medicare and Medicaid Services. Available at http://www.cms.hhs.gov/medicare/hcpcs/codpayproc.asp. Accessed September 26, 2004.

[8]Agreement: The Department of Health and Human Services, Health Care Financing Administration, and American Medical Association. Available at http://www.aapsonline.org/aaps/medicare/hctaama.txt. Accessed September 25, 2004.

[9]Letter from Senator Trent Lott (R-Miss.) to Health and Human Services Secretary Tommy G. Thompson, July 27, 2001. Available at: http://www.aapsonline.org. Accessed September 25, 2004.

[10]Medicare Intermediary Manual Part 3. Available at: http://www.cms.hhs.gov/manuals/13_int/a3605.asp. Accessed September 25, 2004.

[11]Department of Health and Human Services, Health Information Policy Council. Uniform Hospital Discharge Data Set (UHDDS). Washington, DC: 1984.

[12]Top 200 Level I CPT Codes CY 2002. Centers for Medicare and Medicaid Services. Available at: http://www.cms.hhs.gov/statistics/feeforservice/top200L1cptbyservices02.asp. Accessed July 9, 2004.

[13]Washington Administrative Code. WAC 388-531-1850. Payment methodology for physician-related services; CPT/HCPCS Modifiers. Available at: http://www.leg.wa.gov/WAC/index. Accessed September 26, 2004.

[14]American Medical Association. *Current Procedural Terminology 2004.* Chicago: AMA Press; 2004.

[15]Utah Medicaid Provider Manual. Division of Health Care Financing. Available at: http://www.health.state.ut.us/medicaid/phystoc.pdf. Accessed September 27, 2004.

[16]American Medical Association. *Current Procedural Terminology 2004.* Chicago: AMA Press; 2004.

[17]Alternative Billing Codes. Available at:
http://www.alternativelink.com/ali/abc_codes/wiify.asp. Accessed September 28, 2004.

[18]Nirschl R. Return to CPT 1991 E&M Billing System. *Bulletin of the American Academy of Orthopaedic Surgeons.* 2001; 49. Available at
http://www.liu.edu/cwis/cwp/library/workshop/citama.htm. Accessed September 28, 2004.

[19]King MS. Expert agreement in Current Procedural Terminology evaluation and management coding. *Archives of Internal Medicine.* 2002; v162 (3): 316–20.

[20]King MS. Accuracy of CPT evaluation and management coding by family physicians. *Journal American Board of Family Practice.* 2001; May-Jun: 184–92.

CHAPTER 4

How Codes Are Used for Reimbursement

The Price Is Right

When you go to the grocery store and purchase a can of beans, you are pretty certain that you are being charged the same price as everyone else, the price that is posted on the shelf. If you pick a different brand the price may be higher or lower, but once again the price will be the same for everyone. But wait a minute—if you have a supermarket discount card for the clerk to scan, your price after the discount could be less.

Healthcare prices work the same way. If you are a self-pay patient with no insurance, you will be billed the full price and expected to pay it. If you have medical insurance, your insurance company will be billed the same price but will pay less, due to contractual agreements with the providers. If you are able to qualify for a public assistance health insurance program due to your income level, the bill will still be the same, but that program will also pay less than the full amount.

Here's what the reimbursement for your surgeon's bill for your appendectomy might look like:

Procedure: Appendectomy

CPT code billed: 44950 Appendectomy

Surgeon's charge: $1250

If you are a self-pay patient with no insurance, you will be expected to pay the $1250.

If you have Medicare, the payment amounts will look like this:

Insurance: Medicare

Surgeon's charge: $1250

Fee schedule amount: $555

Medicare payment: 80% × $555 = $444

Patient co-insurance: 20% × $555 = $111

What happens to the other $695 ($1250–$555) that nobody is paying for? This amount is known as "contractual allowance." In exchange for being a Medicare provider and receiving payments from Medicare, the physician has in essence entered into a "contract" to accept what Medicare pays. The contractual allowance is the difference between the physician's charge and the amount he has agreed to accept. Even if you have secondary insurance that covers what Medicare doesn't pay, it will only pay your 20%; it will not pay the contractual allowance.

If you have a commercial insurance carrier, the payment might look like this:

Surgeon's charge: $1250

Insurance: Commercial Express

Fee schedule amount: $600

Insurance payment: 80% × $600 = $480

Patient co-insurance: 20% × $600 = $120

Contractual allowance: $650

If your insurance is a health maintenance organization (HMO) or preferred provider organization (PPO), you may have a limit on the amount you have to pay out of pocket—usually a flat rate. In that case, the payment could be:

Surgeon's charge:	$1250
Insurance:	HMO Hometown
Fee schedule amount:	$600
Patient co-pay for surgery:	$100
Insurance payment:	$500
Contractual allowance:	$650

Hospitals also have charges that are often two to four times what they expect to collect from insurers and managed care plans. One of the reasons for this is that hospitals routinely quantify the amount of bad debt and charity care they provide. This helps with fund raising and is used to meet charitable obligations. However, valuing these at full charge greatly overestimates the amount of bad debt and charity care actually provided. Patients who still pay full charges are those with health savings accounts, foreign patients, and the uninsured. This is known as cost shifting. In most hospitals, only three percent of total revenue comes from patients who are uninsured, primarily because they are unable to pay. Almost half of all personal bankruptcies are related to medical bills.[1] Hospitals and other providers can, and do, turn accounts over to collection agencies, garnish wages, and file property liens in order to collect.

Hospitals have come under increasing criticism of their practices with regard to uninsured patients. In February, 2004, the United States Department of Health and Human Services (HHS) clarified its position on charges. Previously, the industry interpretation of government regulations about charges was that all patients had to be billed using the same schedule of charges. The new interpretation offers more flexibility to hospitals wanting to offer discounts to certain patients. HHS clarified that hospitals may develop their own indigency programs with their own definitions, but maintained the stipulation that the criteria must be applied uniformly to Medicare and non-Medicare patients. The result of these changes is that uninsured patients may get the same types of discounts that large payers receive via the contractual allowance.

Geographic location also makes a difference in the amount of reimbursement to both physicians and facility providers. Although Medicare is thought of as a national program, the methods used to calculate reimbursement take into account what is known as a Geographic Practice Cost Index (GPCI, pronounced "gypsy"). Office space is cheaper in Mississippi than in Boston, and the cost of malpractice insurance also varies from state to state. Each CPT code has a relative value (RVU) associated with it. The RVU is multiplied times the GPCI to get the fee schedule amount for a specific area. The Medicare fee schedule has to be budget-neutral, meaning that the total expenditure on health care cannot change. That means that if the value of one procedure code goes up, one or more of the others must go down.

Staking a Claim

Regardless of the type of insurance, almost all reimbursement to healthcare providers and facilities is based on procedure and diagnosis codes. Payers receive this information on a claim form, submitted either on paper or through electronic means.

There are two types of claim forms used by different types of providers. The CMS-1500 claim form is used by physicians, and mid-level providers who are billing independently, while the UB-92 claim form is used by hospitals, home health agencies, ambulance services, rehab facilities, dialysis clinics, and other facilities.

CMS-1500

This form has space for four diagnosis codes and six procedure codes (Fig 4-1). A unique feature of the CMS-1500 is the ability to link a procedure code to one of the four diagnosis codes. This is important in providing medically necessary justification for procedures performed. An example of this situation would be a patient brought to the emergency department after a traffic accident. The patient has a closed fracture of the radius, a bone in the arm. The fracture is treated with closed reduction and casting. However, the patient is also experiencing chest pain, and an electrocardiogram is performed to assess the condition of the patient's heart. The diagnosis codes listed on the claim form are for closed fracture, radius, and a second code for chest pain. Under normal circumstances, a third-party payer would not think that an EKG was medically necessary for an arm fracture. However, if the diagnosis of chest pain has been linked to the EKG procedure code, that will tell the payer the real reason for the EKG, which should then be paid.

The line on which each procedure (CPT or HCPCS code) is reported also has columns for the date(s) of service, place of service, type of service, up to three modifiers, the diagnosis code link, the charge for the service, and the number of days or times (units) the procedure was performed.

The 1500 form also has spaces for the provider's identification and tax ID number, patient demographic and insurance information, referring physician information required for consultations and diagnostic testing, and other information related to processing the claim and determining whether or not it will be paid.

UB-92 Form

The UB-92 (Fig. 4-2) form has space for more diagnosis codes than the CMS 1500 form (principal diagnosis plus 8 others as compared to 4 on the CMS 1500). However, it is not possible to link the procedures to a specific diagnosis. There is also room for

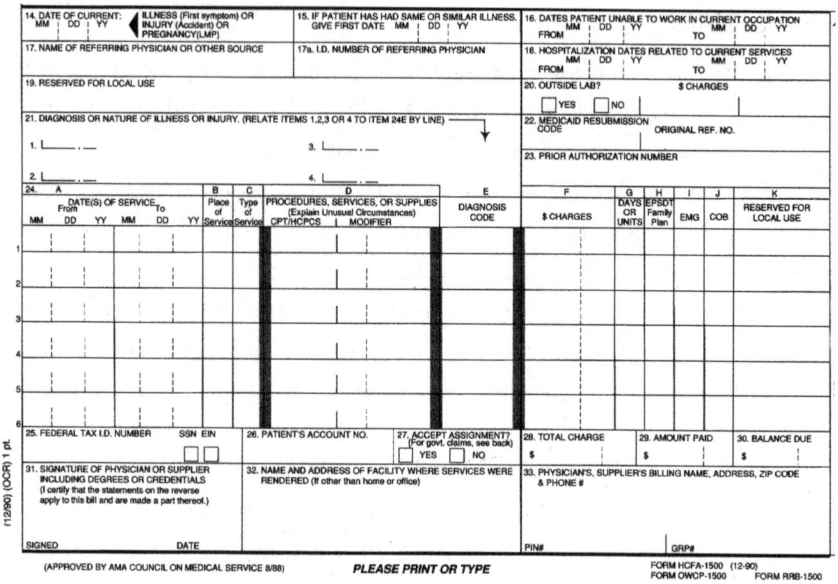
14. DATE OF CURRENT: MM | DD | YY — ILLNESS (First symptom) OR INJURY (Accident) OR PREGNANCY(LMP)
15. IF PATIENT HAS HAD SAME OR SIMILAR ILLNESS. GIVE FIRST DATE MM | DD | YY
16. DATES PATIENT UNABLE TO WORK IN CURRENT OCCUPATION MM | DD | YY FROM TO
17. NAME OF REFERRING PHYSICIAN OR OTHER SOURCE
17a. I.D. NUMBER OF REFERRING PHYSICIAN
18. HOSPITALIZATION DATES RELATED TO CURRENT SERVICES MM | DD | YY FROM TO
19. RESERVED FOR LOCAL USE
20. OUTSIDE LAB? YES NO $ CHARGES
21. DIAGNOSIS OR NATURE OF ILLNESS OR INJURY. (RELATE ITEMS 1,2,3 OR 4 TO ITEM 24E BY LINE)
1. 2. 3. 4.
22. MEDICAID RESUBMISSION CODE ORIGINAL REF. NO.
23. PRIOR AUTHORIZATION NUMBER
24. A DATE(S) OF SERVICE From To MM DD YY MM DD YY | B Place of Service | C Type of Service | D PROCEDURES, SERVICES, OR SUPPLIES (Explain Unusual Circumstances) CPT/HCPCS MODIFIER | E DIAGNOSIS CODE | F $ CHARGES | G DAYS OR UNITS | H EPSDT Family Plan | I EMG | J COB | K RESERVED FOR LOCAL USE
1 2 3 4 5 6
25. FEDERAL TAX I.D. NUMBER SSN EIN
26. PATIENT'S ACCOUNT NO.
27. ACCEPT ASSIGNMENT? (For govt. claims, see back) YES NO
28. TOTAL CHARGE $
29. AMOUNT PAID $
30. BALANCE DUE $
31. SIGNATURE OF PHYSICIAN OR SUPPLIER INCLUDING DEGREES OR CREDENTIALS (I certify that the statements on the reverse apply to this bill and are made a part thereof.)
SIGNED DATE
32. NAME AND ADDRESS OF FACILITY WHERE SERVICES WERE RENDERED (If other than home or office)
33. PHYSICIAN'S, SUPPLIER'S BILLING NAME, ADDRESS, ZIP CODE & PHONE #
PIN# GRP#
(12/90) (OCR) 1 pt.
(APPROVED BY AMA COUNCIL ON MEDICAL SERVICE 8/88) PLEASE PRINT OR TYPE FORM HCFA-1500 (12-90) FORM OWCP-1500 FORM RRB-1500

Figure 4-1 CMS-1500 Claim form (partial)

the principal procedure and 5 others, with a date space adjacent to each procedure code. There is a draft replacement for the UB-92, known as the UB-04. The implementation date for this form is not known at the time of publication. It also has 6 procedure code spaces, but has room for 18 diagnosis codes.

In addition to the reported diagnosis and procedure codes, the UB-92 uses revenue codes to lump together the charges for different categories of services, such as radiology, IV solutions, and drugs. The claim form contains the revenue codes with the number of service units for each and the total charge. The only time that individual procedures are itemized on a UB-92 is for hospital outpatient procedures paid under prospective payment (see Payment Methodologies later in this chapter). Appendix D contains a list of the major groups of revenue codes.

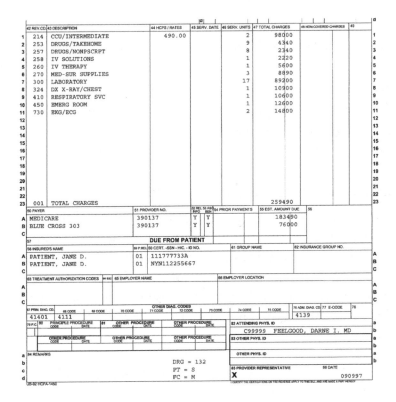

42 REV.CD	43 DESCRIPTION	44 HCPS / RATES	45 SERV. DATE	46 SERV. UNITS	47 TOTAL CHARGES	48 NON-COVERED CHARGES	49
1	214	CCU/INTERMEDIATE	490.00		2	98000		1
2	253	DRUGS/TAKEHOME			9	4340		2
3	257	DRUGS/NONPSCRPT			8	2340		3
4	258	IV SOLUTIONS			1	2220		4
5	260	IV THERAPY			1	5600		5
6	270	MED-SUR SUPPLIES			3	8890		6
7	300	LABORATORY			17	89200		7
8	324	DX X-RAY/CHEST			1	10900		8
9	410	RESPIRATORY SVC			1	10600		9
10	450	EMERG ROOM			1	12600		10
11	730	EKG/ECG			2	14800		11

(Rows 12–23 blank)

| 23 | 001 | TOTAL CHARGES | | | | 259490 | |

50 PAYER		51 PROVIDER NO.	52 REL INFO	53 ASG BEN	54 PRIOR PAYMENTS	55 EST. AMOUNT DUE	56
A	MEDICARE	390137	Y	Y		183490	
B	BLUE CROSS 303	390137	Y	Y		76000	
C							

| 57 | | DUE FROM PATIENT |

58 INSURED'S NAME	59 P.REL	60 CERT. -SBN - HIC. - ID NO.	61 GROUP NAME	62 INSURANCE GROUP NO.
A	PATIENT, JANE D.	01	111777733A		A
B	PATIENT, JANE D.	01	NYN112255667		B
C					C

63 TREATMENT AUTHORIZATION CODES	64 ESC	65 EMPLOYER NAME	66 EMPLOYER LOCATION
A				A
B				B
C				C

67 PRIN. DIAG. CD	68 CODE	69 CODE	70 CODE	OTHER DIAG. CODES 71 CODE	72 CODE	73 CODE	74 CODE	75 CODE	76 ADM. DIAG. CD	77 E-CODE	76
41401	4111								4139		

79 P.C	80 PRINCIPLE PROCEDURE CODE / DATE	81	OTHER PROCEDURE CODE / DATE	OTHER PROCEDURE CODE / DATE	OTHER PROCEDURE CODE / DATE	82 ATTENDING PHYS. ID	a
						C99999 FEELGOOD, DARNE I. MD	b

OTHER PROCEDURE CODE / DATE	OTHER PROCEDURE CODE / DATE	OTHER PROCEDURE CODE / DATE	83 OTHER PHYS. ID	a
				b

84 REMARKS	OTHER PHYS. ID	a
a		b
b	DRG = 132	
c	PT = S	85 PROVIDER REPRESENTATIVE 86 DATE
d	FC = M	X 090997

UB-92 HCFA-1450

Figure 4-2   UB-92 Claim form (partial)

Claims Submission

Claims are sent from the provider or facility to the payer via one of three methods:

- Paper: Although the days of a clerk typing out a claim form are almost gone, there are still providers who submit claims manually, on paper forms. CMS requires all payers except facilities with fewer than 25 full-time equivalent employees (FTE's) and other providers with fewer than 10 FTE's to file initial claims electronically.[2]

- Electronic via billing entity or clearinghouse: These businesses submit claims on behalf of providers. They may format billing data to meet the needs of individual payers and perform edits on the billing data to verify completion of all required fields.

- Electronic direct: Electronic submission of claims has the advantage of speeding up the payment process. It requires less processing by the payer than manual paper claims and usually employs front-end edits to assure correct or "clean" claims.

Claims Processing and Adjudication

Once the insurance company or other payer has received the claim information, either electronically or on paper, it processes the claim. This can involve extracting data from the claim, scanning claims for retention, and validation of specific data elements. Checking the claim at this point may result in rejection of the claim for reasons having nothing to do with the diagnosis and procedure codes, such as:

- Payer can't identify the patient as being insured with his or her company
- Patient's coverage with the payer terminated before the date of service on the claim
- The time limit for filing the claim has expired
- Duplicate claim

The claims adjudication process involves review of the claim to make sure that the service provided is covered under the specific insurance plan, and that all required information is available. Adjudication of physician or other professional services claims occurs at the line-item level, charge by charge by charge. One line of a claim may be paid, while others are rejected. In addition to deciding whether or not a specific charge will be paid, the adjudication process also determines how much will be paid. The payment amount is based on the fee schedule amount for that procedure, the place of service, and any applicable contract stipulations. Another factor will be whether or not you, the patient, have met your deductible for the current year. If not, you will be liable for the portion of the reimbursed amount that is less than or equal to your deductible. You will be paying the doctor instead of the insurance company paying the doctor.

Many, many errors on the part of the payer are possible during the claims adjudication process:

- Newly enrolled individuals not yet loaded into the company's system
- Errors in names, dates of birth, addresses, and other demographic information
- Incorrect rekeying of claims information by the payer into their own system
- System programming errors
- Inability of system to recognize modifiers justifying additional payment
- Systems not updated to new diagnosis and procedure codes
- Prior authorizations for services not loaded into system
- Payment amounts specified in current contracts not updated

Claims that require additional information or that need correction of errors are "pended." The provider is notified of the reason why the claim is pended and what needs to be done. Claims that complete the adjudication process are referred to as "finalized claims." Finalized claims can be one of three things: paid, rejected, or denied. A payment advice or remittance advice notice is sent to the provider notifying them of the outcome. A check is also sent for paid claims.

The Rejection Puzzle

Figuring out why a claim has been rejected is often difficult and frustrating. Prior to 2003, there were approximately 4,000 different remittance advice codes in use. Many had the same meanings, with minor differences in wording. The Health Insurance Portability and Accountability Act (HIPAA) of 1996 contained an Administrative Simplification provision that addressed the need, not only for standardized code sets for diagnoses and procedures, but also standard transactions such as remittance advice codes. As a result, the thousands of remittance advice codes were condensed into a little more than 200. Appendix E contains the most commonly used reason codes.

If you receive an explanation of benefits indicating that a service was denied, it is important to work with your doctor to determine why. In some cases, the insurer may be requesting additional information from you. This could happen in the case of an auto accident, where the auto insurance is supposed to pay first. Another situation like this would be if you were to fall on private property and injure yourself. The property owner's liability insurance might be the primary payer. You and your doctor are both interested in making sure he is paid, so it is essential that you cooperate in efforts to resolve denials and rejections.

Medical Necessity

Determination of medical necessity involves comparing the procedure being billed to the diagnosis submitted. If you receive a denial notice from the payer that the procedure was "not medically necessary" it means that your payer does not think the procedure or test was justified for the diagnosis given. Medicare carriers publish what are known as "Local Medical Review Policies" (LMRPs) that contain lists of diagnosis codes that validate procedures such as EKGs, chest x-rays, and others. If your diagnosis is not on the list, your claim will be rejected. Screening exams, such as Pap smears, mammograms, and colonoscopies, are also subject to frequency limitations dictating how often they will be paid.

If the provider of the service knows in advance that a service is likely to be deemed not medically necessary, they can ask the patient to sign an Advance Beneficiary Notice (ABN) in which the patient acknowledges the possibility the claim won't be paid and agrees to be financially liable himself. ABNs must be specific to the service provided; they can't be blanket forms covering any and all services. Without an ABN signed before the service occurs, the provider cannot bill the beneficiary if the claim is rejected.

Some services are never covered, such as cosmetic surgery. Patients can be billed for non-covered procedures without an ABN.

Instead of rejecting the claim, some payers will "downcode" it based on the diagnosis. For example, if your doctor bills a Level 4 established office visit code (99214) when he sees you for your sore throat, your insurance company may decide that a sore throat will never be more complicated than a Level 3 service. In fact, they may implement a process of rejecting all Level 4 and 5 claims and require physicians to submit additional documentation in order to be paid. This practice penalizes not only physicians who might use the higher level codes without clinical justification, but all other physicians who actually document according to the requirements of the higher levels. The American Medical Association (AMA) has developed policies strongly opposing downcoding.[3]

Payment Methodologies

Just as the coding systems are different, the payment methodologies for inpatient hospital, outpatient hospital, and professional claims differ. Many payers follow the lead of Medicare once it has implemented a specific payment system.

Fee for Service

The most traditional payment mechanism is known as fee for service. It's simple. A service is billed using a CPT or ICD-9-CM procedure code. The payer has a fee schedule with a set reimbursement amount for each service they cover. The provider gets the fee schedule amount less any deductible or co-insurance owed by the patient.

Most physician services are paid according to a fee schedule. Clinical laboratory services are paid based on a laboratory fee schedule, and ambulance services on an ambulance fee schedule.

Reasonable Cost or Cost Based

Under this method, providers or facilities submit an annual cost report, detailing the expenses of running their businesses.

The rules for completing the cost report are extensive. They include data on bed utilization, salaries by cost center, expenses by cost center, indirect costs related to items such as medical education, cost-to-charge ratios (how much it costs to provide a service per dollar charged), capital expenditures, and other items. In many cases the facility has been receiving periodic interim payments from the payer throughout the year, and the cost report is then used to "settle" or reconcile the costs to the payments already received. For Medicare, the cost reports are submitted to the Fiscal Intermediary (FI) which reviews and/or audits the cost report and then submits it to the Centers for Medicare and Medicaid Services (CMS) for reporting.

The periodic interim payments (PIP) are available to inpatient hospitals, skilled nursing facility services, hospice services, and critical access hospitals (small hospitals in rural areas that are needed to assure access to healthcare for local populations). Facilities are supposed to self-monitor their PIP payments to assure they are not receiving overpayments, and penalties are in place if overpayment exceeds two percent of the total in two consecutive fiscal reporting periods.

Prospective Payment—Inpatient Hospital

Government health planners who were interested in restraining the costs of Medicare, Medicaid, and other insurance programs realized that cost-based reimbursement was a sure way to eat up dollars faster and faster. In order to change hospital behavior to encourage more efficient management of medical care, Medicare introduced hospital inpatient prospective payment in 1983. Using a system developed by Yale University in the 1970s, reimbursement to hospitals was based on Diagnosis Related Groups (DRGs). Data already appearing on the claim form is used to assign each patient discharge into a DRG:

- Principal diagnosis (see definition in Chapter 2)
- Complications and Comorbidities (CCs)
- Surgical procedures
- Age
- Gender
- Discharge disposition (died, transferred, went home)

The principal diagnosis, the reason the patient was admitted to the hospital, determines to which Major Diagnostic Category (MDC) the case will be assigned. There are 25 MDCs, based on body organ system or disease:

MDC 1	Diseases and disorders of the nervous system
MDC 2	Diseases and disorders of the eye
MDC 3	Diseases and disorders of the ear, nose, mouth, and throat
MDC 4	Diseases and disorders of the respiratory system
MDC 5	Diseases and disorders of the circulatory system
MDC 6	Diseases and disorders of the digestive system
MDC 7	Diseases and disorders of the hepatobiliary system and pancreas
MDC 8	Diseases and disorders of the musculoskeletal system and connective tissue
MDC 9	Diseases and disorders of the skin, subcutaneous tissue, and breast
MDC 10	Endocrine, nutritional, and metabolic diseases and disorders
MDC 11	Diseases and disorders of the kidney and urinary tract
MDC 12	Diseases and disorders of the male reproductive system
MDC 13	Diseases and disorders of the female reproductive system
MDC 14	Pregnancy, childbirth, and the puerperium
MDC 15	Newborns and other neonates with conditions originating in the perinatal period
MDC 16	Diseases and disorders of blood, blood forming organs, immunologic disorders
MDC 17	Myeloproliferative diseases and disorders, poorly differentiated neoplasms
MDC 18	Infectious and parasitic diseases, systemic or unspecified sites

MDC 19	Mental diseases and disorders
MDC 20	Alcohol / drug use and alcohol / drug induced organic mental disorders
MDC 21	Injuries, poisonings, and toxic effects of drugs
MDC 22	Burns
MDC 23	Factors influencing health status and other contacts with health services
MDC 24	Multiple significant trauma
MDC 25	Human immunodeficiency virus infections[4]

Within each MDC, the next partition is based on whether or not a significant procedure was performed, and whether or not the patient had complications or comorbidities. Patient age and length of stay in the hospital may also affect DRG assignment. There are over 500 DRGs. Those without significant procedures are known as "medical" DRGs while those with significant procedures are "surgical" DRGs.

Once a DRG has been assigned, the determination of the reimbursement amount can start. Each DRG has a relative weight assigned to it. Patients in a given DRG are assumed to have similar conditions, receive similar services, and use similar amounts of hospital resources. The prospective payment system is based on paying the average cost to treat patients in that DRG. The DRG weights are adjusted annually. As might be expected, the more complex the DRG the higher the weight.

The DRG for a heart transplant has a weight of more than 19.0, while the DRG for an uncomplicated appendectomy is less than 1.0. In order to calculate the reimbursement rate, the weight for the DRG is multiplied times a base payment amount, which has geographical wage and cost of living factors built in. In addition, if the hospital is a teaching facility it will receive additional Indirect Medical Education funds. If it treats a disproportionate (high) percentage of Medicare patients, it will receive extra funding as a result.

Some patients are known as "outliers." This means that the charges for their care greatly exceed the average amount considered normal for a particular DRG. Complications, additional unplanned surgery, or other reasons can cause an outlier. For fiscal year 2005, the charges for the outlier must exceed the DRG payment amount by $35,085. Let's assume that a patient was admitted for a cholecystectomy (removal of the gallbladder) with exploration of the common bile duct. This case would fall under DRG 196 and the reimbursement amount would be around $9,115 depending on the geographic location of the hospital. In order to get extra payment over and above the $9,115, the patient's charges would have to total at least $44,200. Until the charges reached that point, the hospital would not get one extra dime. If a patient is admitted because of a heart attack and falls out of bed, breaking his leg, the hospital will not get any additional money for the extra days that patient will spend, unless he eventually becomes an outlier.

Like many other aspects of healthcare reimbursement, the ability to code completely to reach the correct DRG depends largely on physician documentation. Coders are not allowed to make assumptions about what might have been. The presence of laboratory results in a chart indicating the culture of bacteria, or a chest x-ray consistent with pneumonia, cannot be used for coding purposes unless the physician documents their existence. Since documentation under prospective payment systems equals better coding equals higher reimbursement, physicians have been "urged" to improve by including additional complications and comorbidities. The following list represents diagnoses that can make a payment difference in surgical cases:

- Acute blood loss anemia
- Angina
- Atrial fibrillation
- Congestive heart failure (CHF)
- Dehydration
- Hematuria (blood in urine)
- Ileus (intestinal slowdown)

- Phelibitis (IV site)
- Respiratory failure
- Sepsis (infection in the blood)

Surgeons have been told that documenting these complications demonstrates how sick their patients are. However, documenting these conditions in addition to the principal diagnosis also means more money for the hospital.

Prospective Payment—Ambulatory Surgical Centers

Ambulatory Surgical Centers (ASCs) have been covered under Medicare since 1982. Their primary function is to perform surgical procedures that can be done safely in an outpatient setting, but require a higher level of service than is normally found in a doctor's office. ASC procedures are generally called "day surgery." The patient undergoes surgery, receives recovery nursing services, and then goes home the same day.

Unlike the DRG system, the ASC prospective payments are based only on the procedures. There are only nine procedure groups, each with a specific payment rate. If more than one procedure is performed, the ASC receives full payment for the procedure with the highest rate, while the additional procedures are paid at fifty percent.

Like the DRG system, the ASC rates are updated annually, and newly approved procedure codes are categorized and added to the payment scheme. Items covered under prospective payment are operative nursing, recovery room, anesthetic agents, drugs, and supplies.

Prospective Payment—Skilled Nursing Facilities

These facilities care for patients who require the skilled services of licensed nursing staff, or skilled rehabilitation. In order to qualify for Medicare coverage of skilled nursing, the patient must have been hospitalized for at least three days prior to being admitted to the skilled facility, and must be admitted within 30 days after being discharged from the hospital. Skilled Nursing Facilities (SNF) were paid under a retrospective cost-based system until July 1998. Since then, a payment scheme based on the acuity or illness of the patient has been used. It measures the intensity of care required and the amount of resources used.

Resource Utilization Groups (RUGS) are similar to DRGs in concept. Each facility is paid a daily rate based on the needs of individual Medicare patients, with an adjustment for local labor costs. Forty-four individual classifications are found within the seven major RUGS categories:

- Rehabilitation (14 classifications)
- Extensive Services (3 classifications)
- Special Care (3 classifications)
- Clinically Complex (6 classifications)
- Behavior Only (4 classifications)
- Decreased Physical Function (10 classifications)

The Resident Assessment Instrument (RAI) is used to gather and document information about the patient. In addition to information about the patient's medical condition, the RAI includes a number of items covering functional and social activities, customary habits or practices at home, and psychosocial well-being. The data from the RAI is used to classify the patient into a RUGS group and payment to the facility is based on the group.

Prospective Payment—Home Health Agency

To receive home health services covered by Medicare, a patient must be homebound, have a need for skilled nursing care or services such as physical therapy or speech therapy, be under a plan of care periodically recertified by a physician, and receive care from a Medicare certified home health agency. Agencies receive a lump sum payment to cover the first 60 days of home health care, based on the needs of the patient. In 2004, this sum was about $2250 plus market basket and local wage adjustments. A data set on home health agency clients, OASIS (Outcome and Assessment Information Set), is the basis for the payment calculation. OASIS also includes data on outcomes and quality measures, which are published on the CMS website for public review.

If the home health agency is well managed and works efficiently, it can keep any profit it makes from the prospective payments by lowering costs per visit, or by reducing the number of services while still maintaining a quality outcome for the patient.

Prospective Payment—Hospital Outpatient

In August, 2000, Medicare implemented a prospective payment system for hospital outpatient services. Similar to DRGs for inpatients, this system is known as Ambulatory Payment Classifications, or APCs. Like DRGs, each APC contains clinically similar conditions using the same level of facility resources. There are approximately 800 APCs, including procedure-based, medical, and ancillary such as laboratory or radiology testing. The unit of service for an APC is one calendar day. Unlike DRGs, hospitals may be paid a prospective rate for more than one APC per day, depending on the circumstances of the encounter.

APC payment for a given procedure includes facility charges, drugs, supplies, and time. Some items are paid separately, on a "pass-through" basis, primarily because they may have been developed too recently to have been taken into consideration during the establishment of the APC rates.

The Effect of Payment Methods on Coding

Long ago and far away, coding began as a systematic method of tracking disease incidence. Its entanglement with reimbursement systems has greatly increased its importance within health care organizations. For years, the hospital medical record departments where coding occurred were dusty file rooms that existed primarily because of documentation-related regulatory requirements. With the implementation of inpatient prospective payment via DRGs in 1983, coding made a difference in reimbursement for the first time. Coders were elevated out of the dark basements into the financial limelight. Medical record departments were transformed into "health information management departments."

With the newly focused attention on coding, and the potential dollars to be made from using the "right" codes, came the perils of ethical dilemmas and pressure for coders to contribute to the financial success of their employers. Join us in Chapter 5 as we look at Fraud and Abuse.

References

[1]Anderson G. A Review of Hospital Billing and Collection Practices. Testimony before the Committee on Energy and Commerce, United States House of Representatives, 6/24/04. Available at: http://energycommerce.house.gov/108/Hearings/06242004hearing1299/Anderson2095.htm. Accessed October 2, 2004.

[2]Centers for Medicare and Medicaid Services (CMS). Publication 100-04, Medicare Claims Processing. Transmittal 44, 12/19/03. Available at: http://www.cms.hhs.gov/manuals/pm_trans/R44CP.pdf. Accessed October 3, 2004.

[3]American Medical Association. American Medical Association Model Managed Care Contract: Supplement 6. Downcoding and Bundling of Claims: What Physicians Need to Know About These Payment Problems. 2002. Available at: http://www.ama-assn.org/ama1/pub/upload/mm/368/supplement6.pdf. Accessed October 1, 2004.

[4]Centers for Medicare and Medicaid Services (CMS). Acute Inpatient Prospective Payment System. Available at http://www.cms.hhs.gov/providers/hipps/background.asp. Accessed October 4, 2004.

CHAPTER 5

Coding for Dollars

Healthcare Fraud and Abuse

As funding and reimbursement for healthcare cover less and less of the cost of providing care, the temptation to find "loopholes" in the reimbursement systems grows.

The United States Department of Health and Human Services (HHS) established a Fraud and Abuse Control Program, effective January 1, 1997. The Office of Inspector General (OIG) carries out nationwide audits, investigations, and inspections, in order to protect the integrity of HHS programs. Included as subjects of the investigatory efforts would be any healthcare program that receives and distributes federal funds. OIG also has the authority to investigate hospitals, pharmaceutical manufacturers, third-party medical billing companies, ambulance companies, physician practices, nursing facilities, home health agencies, clinical laboratories, hospices, and companies that supply durable medical equipment, prosthetics and orthotics. In other words, almost anybody and everybody associated with healthcare. The OIG can also involve the Federal Bureau of Investigation (FBI) or other federal agencies as needed to assist with investigations.

The HHS OIG is primarily concerned with compliance, which means establishing a business environment that complies with principles of business practice, as identified by the OIG, that are intended to increase the stability of the Medical Trust Fund by reducing fraud and abuse in the claims process. Fraud can occur due to deliberately unethical behavior, or because of mistakes and ignorance of the law.

The OIG has the force of law behind its investigations and prosecutions. Some of the laws it enforces cover business processes and relationships:

- The "Stark" laws (named after Congressman Pete Stark of California) address financial interests of physicians in companies or services to which they refer patients or submit claims. An extensive list of designated services is covered.

- The Anti-Kickback Statute prohibits the knowing payment of anything of value to influence referral of federal healthcare program business.

- Patient anti-dumping statutes. These laws were developed as a result of the days in which hospitals would do "financial triage," where the poor and uninsured would be put back in the ambulance and sent to the public hospital. It requires that any patient presenting for emergency care be given an appropriate medical screening exam to determine whether they have an emergency condition. If such a condition exists, the patient must be stabilized before being discharged or transferred.

Civil monetary penalties may be imposed on corporations or individuals found to have violated federal regulations related to healthcare financial transactions. The maximum civil monetary penalty is currently $10,000 per item or service, with the possibility of triple penalties in some instances. Some of the actions for which civil monetary penalties may be imposed are:

- Submitting a claim or claims that the person knows or should know is for an item or service that is not medically necessary

- Failing to provide an itemized statement when requested by a Medicare benficiary
- Unsolicited telephone contacts with Medicare beneficiaries regarding furnishing covered durable medical equipment
- Billing for an assistant at cataract surgery
- Charging a beneficiary for completing and submitting claim forms
- Charging a Medicare beneficiary more than the limiting charge (nonparticipating physicians or suppliers)
- Hiring an individual who has been excluded from participation in federal healthcare programs[1]

Exclusion from federal healthcare programs can occur as a result of convictions for program-related fraud and patient abuse, licensing board actions, and default on health educational assistance loans. The exclusion extends beyond direct patient care or billing and claims to any type of receipt of federal funds, even a salary for serving as an administrative functionary. Employers who knowingly hire excluded individuals may themselves be fined or prosecuted. A list of excluded individuals and entities is available on the HHS OIG website. During the first half of fiscal year 2004, the OIG excluded 1,544 individuals and entities from participating in federal healthcare programs. Some of the reasons for exclusion were:

- Unproven opiate detox program. The procedure is not medically established; six patients died and others were hospitalized after undergoing the procedure.
- Child molestation
- False blood tests. The provider used blood drawn from his employees to submit false claims.
- Illegal prescription of controlled substances[2]

One of the ways the OIG gets information on questionable practices is through "whistleblower" suits. Qui tam litigation allows private citizens to act on the government's behalf in filing lawsuits alleging that an individual or corporation has violated the federal False Claims Act. Anyone who has information about the practices of a provider can be a whistleblower. In some cases, that individual turns out to be a current or former employee of the organization being investigated. The whistleblower may receive up to 25% of the money the government recovers.

Settlements of fraud cases during the past few years are dramatic:

- Seven of 27 qui tam suits filed against HCA—The Health Company, were settled in 2001 with the company agreeing to pay $840 million in criminal and civil fines and penalties. Other allegations included the maintenance of two different sets of cost reports.

- In June 2002, Tenet Healthcare Corporation paid the government $55.8 million to settle a series of Medicare fraud charges, some initiated by whistleblowers. They included:

  ○ $17 million for overcharging for laboratory services in 139 hospitals

  ○ $10 million for overbilling for rehab services and filing false cost reports

  ○ $29 million for billing and cost report violations for home health services

The same company agreed in August 2003 to pay another $54 million to settle a government case in which doctors at a Tenet-owned hospital performed hundreds of invasive heart procedures that were not medically necessary. The company admitted no wrongdoing and no criminal charges were filed.

- During the first half of fiscal year 2004, the OIG tallied over $1.5 billion in audit and investigative receivables, including:

  ○ Another $631 million from HCA to resolve remaining civil claims and $250 million to resolve administrative overpayments in connection with cost reports

- School-based health services improper claims for $172 million in New York State
- Allegations against Abbott Laboratories of kickbacks to purchasers of enteral nutrition products - $615 million
- A Michigan physician had to repay $242,000 because he routinely billed in excess of 100 nursing home patient visits a day, and had no documentation to support them.
- Personal expenses, including jewelry, flowers, and clothing were claimed on a falsified cost report by a home health agency administrator in Minnesota.
- A licensed clinical social worker in Georgia billed for services in excess of 24 hours a day and submitted over 300 claims for dates of service when he was actually out of town.

Creative methods of obtaining inappropriate reimbursement have included:

- Claiming transferred patients as discharges, thus increasing revenue by $4.7 million at 35 different hospitals in North Carolina[3]
- Increasing charges substantially in order to obtain inappropriate outlier payments for inpatients

Each year, the OIG publishes a work plan to define its areas of focus for the coming year. For 2005, some of the "hot" topics are:

- Medical necessity of inpatient psychiatric stays
- Organ acquisition costs
- Inpatient outlier and other charge-related issues
- Coronary artery stents
- Enhanced payments for home health therapy
- Involvement of skilled nursing facilities in consecutive inpatient hospital stays

- Imaging and laboratory services in nursing homes
- Use of modifier -25
- Care plan oversight
- Prescription drug cards
- Air ambulance services
- Emergency health services for undocumented aliens
- Overprescribing of oxycontin and other psychotropic drugs
- Payments for services provided after beneficiaries' deaths

In addition to auditing and investigating providers of services, the OIG also serves as the internal auditor for HHS programs and identifies existing or potential problems with agency financial matters.

OIG Compliance Guidance

In response to the large number of identified compliance issues, the OIG began issuing Compliance Program Guidance papers for different types of healthcare entities. They contain seven critical components of an effective complicance program:

- Implementing written policies, procedures, and standards of conduct
- Designating a compliance officer and compliance committee
- Conducting effective training and education
- Developing effective lines of communication
- Enforcing standards through well-publicized disciplinary guidelines
- Conducting internal monitoring and auditing
- Responding promptly to detected offenses and developing corrective action

If the healthcare entity implements a compliance program that meets the criteria listed previously, it will be looked upon favorably should a future problem be identified by the OIG, as at least having made the effort.

What Does This Have to Do with Coding?

Think about the implications of a diagnosis or procedure code equal to a certain number of dollars. Do the lightbulbs go on? Is there a huge potential for increasing reimbursement through fraudulent coding? The answer is a most definite "yes."

A survey of American doctors conducted in 2001 indicated that 39% admitted to having used tactics such as exaggerating symptoms, changing billing diagnoses, or reporting signs or symptoms the patients did not have in order to secure additional services felt to be clinically necessary.[4]

Some of the coding-related OIG "hot topics" in the 2005 workplan are:

- DRG coding
- Coding of evaluation and management services
- Use of modifiers with nationally correct coding initiative edits

One of the first signs of inappropriate or fraudulent coding is known as "DRG creep." It can be identified when a hospital's case mix index, or average of the total of the values assigned to all DRGs for that hospital's patients, increases from year to year, or when the incidence of high-severity codes is found at a higher level than the incidence of that severity of disease is found in the population.

Although it would be nice to think that the increase in higher weighted DRGs is due to improved physician documentation in the medical record, it can also be due to increased use of specialized expert software systems that identify potential diagnoses that could be used to maximize reimbursement.

Once the needed diagnosis is identified, a "query form" can be sent to the physician to see if perhaps he "forgot" to document that condition in the chart.

Rules for the use of query forms indicate they cannot lead the physician to document specifically to increase reimbursement. The sticky note illustrated in Figure 5-1 is an example of an inappropriate query.

DRGs often occur in pairs, one without a complication or comorbidity and one with. The latter always pays more.

An example is:

DRG 458: Spinal fusion except cervical without CC

DRG 457: Spinal fusion except cervical with CC

DRG 458 without the complication or comorbidity is worth around $13,000, varying by geographic location and case mix

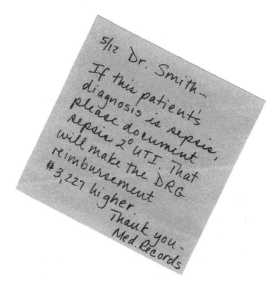

Figure 5-1 Query

index, while adding a complication or comorbidity brings in an additional $4,500. An analysis of 2002 Medicare inpatient data showed that use of complications and comorbidities had generated an additional $100 million in additional prospective payment system revenue for hospitals in that year. Between 2001 and 2002, the rate of coding a complication or comorbidity increased in 16 of 99 code pairs studied the first year to increases in 64 of the same 99 pairs reviewed the second year. From 1998 to 1999, none of the 99 pairs showed an increase in the use of complications and comorbidities.[5]

Other abuses are specificity-related. Coders are not supposed to make assumptions about diagnoses based on lab work or other diagnostic results in the chart. Coding is supposed to be based on physician documentation. However, in some facilities a positive culture report was a signal to coders that a bacterial diagnosis could be assigned, even without physician documentation. In January, 2003, a whistleblower suit brought by a coder at a Tennessee hospital alleged a number of DRG coding violations, including specific instructions to coders to upcode or use complications, even without complete chart documentation. The hospital settled for $2 million and the coder whistleblower received $350,000.

As demonstrated in previous chapters of this book, coding is extremely complex. The rules are different, depending on the site of service, and who is submitting a bill. Because there are areas of coding that are open to interpretation, it is often the case that coding errors are mistakes, not intentional. This can be taken into account by investigators if they see mistakes but not a pattern of "mistakes." An example would be investigation by the OIG into the correct assignment of principal diagnosis codes. According to official diagnosis coding guidelines, when a patient has a urinary tract infection, that code is sequenced first, before the code for the organism. If the order of the codes is switched, a higher weight DRG is assigned. If all the cases of this type in a hospital were sequenced improperly, that facility might be charged with intentional fraud. In another facility, if only a few cases were improperly sequenced, no pattern would be identified and the facility would have to refund money, but it is unlikely that facility would be accused of fraud.[6]

Coders, even in settings such as physician offices, confront ethical dilemmas on a daily basis. As employees, they want to see their organizations succeed financially. As professionals, they want to adhere to the standards of conduct and ethical principles defined by their professional organizations. Appendix C contains the Code of Ethics of the American Health Information Management Association. Section 4.6 specifically addresses the following unethical practices:

- Allowing patterns of retrospective documentation to avoid suspension or increase reimbursement
- Assigning codes without physician documentation
- Coding when documentation does not justify the procedures that have been billed
- Coding an inappropriate level of service
- Miscoding to avoid conflict with others
- Engaging in negligent coding practices

Preventive Measures

Coding managers and others involved in the process of coding for reimbursement purposes should be pro-active in identifying potential risk areas. Comparative data is available for all types of facilities to compare their DRG, APC, or other payment category results to national or regional norms. Using outside auditors to review coding practices and patterns is advisable to increase objectivity. Billing system edits and payer rejection data are good sources of information to prompt educational efforts for coders.

In June 2004, the OIG published Draft Supplemental Compliance Program Guidance for Hospitals. It focuses on activities that are most likely to represent a potential source of liability. It includes the following onerous statements:

"Perhaps the single biggest risk area for hospitals is the preparation and submission of claims or other requests for payment . . . "

"Common and longstanding risks associated with claims preparation and submission include inaccurate or incorrect coding, upcoding, unbundling of services, billing for medically unnecessary services or other services not covered by the relevant health care program, billing for services not provided, duplicate billing, insufficient documentation, and false or fraudulent cost reports."[7]

The need to monitor and improve coding and documentation practices is ongoing and necessary to assure payment accuracy.

References

[1]Centers for Medicare and Medicaid Services. Description of Civil Monetary Penalties (CMPs). Available at: http://www.cms.hhs.gov/providers/fraud/comp2.asp. Accessed October 3, 2004.

[2]Department of Health and Human Services, Office of Inspector General. Semiannual Report to Congress, October 1, 2003 to March 31, 2004. Available at http://oig.hhs.gov/publications/docs/semiannual/2004. Accessed October 14, 2004.

[3]Department of Health and Human Services, Office of Inspector General. Audit A-05-03-000041. Available at: http://oig/hhs.gov/oas/reports/region5/50300041.htm. Accessed October 14, 2004.

[4]Hyman DA. Health care fraud and abuse: market change, social norms, and the trust reposed in the workmen. Journal of Legal Studies, 2001:30; 531–67.

[5]HSS, Inc. Increased Coding of Complications & Comorbidities Generates $100 Million in Additional Hospital Revenue. Available at: http://www.hssweb.com/news/. Accessed October 2, 2004.

[6]Prophet S. Fraud and Abuse Implications for the HIM Professional. Journal of AHIMA 68, No. 4 (1997):52–56.

[7]U.S. Department of Health and Human Services, Office of Inspector General. Draft Supplemental Compliance Guidance for Hospitals. *Federal Register.* Vol. 69, No. 110. Tuesday June 8, 2004: §32012–32032.

Solving Your Healthcare Coding Problems

Most healthcare coding problems affecting patients become evident under two circumstances:

- You are denied <u>for</u> insurance, or
- You are denied <u>by</u> insurance

Get a Life

When you apply for life insurance, the standard application form includes a space for your signature authorizing the company to check your medical information from various sources. One of those sources may be the Medical Information Bureau (MIB, Inc.) It is an association of more than 500 US and Canadian life insurance companies, organized in 1902. It describes its core fraud protection services as protecting "insurers, policyholders, and applicants from attempts to conceal or omit information material to the sound and equitable underwriting of life, health, disability, and long term care insurance."[1]

MIB maintains a database of individuals who have applied for insurance. The database includes information on about 230 medical conditions that indicate the applicant's risk. In addition, other data such as hazardous occupations or adverse driving records are included. When you apply for insurance, the company, with your authorization in hand, can check to see if you have an MIB record, and if so, what your risk factors are. Likewise, if you have an exam in conjunction with your application, information from that exam such as high blood pressure or an abnormal EKG can be added to your MIB record.

You may obtain a copy of your MIB record. There is a small fee for the record, unless you have been turned down for insurance based on MIB as an information source. For more information, contact MIB at (617) 426-3660 or at P.O. Box 105, Essex Station, Boston, MA 02112.

For the Record

If you think that medical information about you is incorrect, you probably need to obtain a copy of your medical record. The Federal Health Insurance Portability and Accountability Act (HIPAA) requires health-care providers, health plans, and healthcare clearinghouses to allow you access to your medical records. There is often a fee for copying medical records. It may be more economical to review the record in person at the doctor's office, hospital, or other facility and then request copies of only the relevant information you need.

Some of the parts of your record that can be helpful in addressing errors or incorrect bills are:

- Face sheet. This form is usually found on inpatient hospital records. It contains your demographic information such as date of birth, address and phone number, insurance policy numbers, and the dates of your admission and discharge. More important, it also contains the principal and other diagnoses, the principal and other procedures, and the diagnosis and procedure codes that were assigned by the hospital. These codes should match up with the codes submitted on claim forms to your insurance company.

- <u>Doctors' orders.</u> Nothing can be done to you or for you without a doctor's order. Physicians order tests, treatments, medications, diets, and nursing interventions such as vital signs or dressing changes. If you are disputing charges on a bill, checking what was billed against the orders in the record may disclose errors.

- <u>Operative report.</u> If you had surgery, the surgeon is required to document the type of operation, the technique used, operative findings, complications, and estimated blood loss. The description of the procedure in the operative report should match the description of the procedure code for which you were billed. If more than one procedure was performed, payers may invoke bundling rules that define which procedures will be paid and which won't.

- <u>History and Physical.</u> This report, known as the "H&P" is the initial assessment of your physical and emotional status as you enter the hospital. It could be important in issues related to medical necessity. Were you sick enough to require hospitalization and the treatments that were ordered?

- <u>Discharge Summary.</u> An account of your hospital course, this report is where the doctor makes his final statement about your diagnoses and procedures and also where plans for your ongoing treatment or follow-up are documented. The diagnoses and procedures here should match up with the face sheet and with any claims submitted to your payer.

How Do Coding Errors Occur?

Medical coding analysts are involved in constant decision-making. Is it this diagnosis or that? Which diagnosis should be principal? Was the procedure bilateral? Did the physician document enough time to code critical care? Even the task of deciphering physician handwriting involves deciding what was actually documented. There are two types of errors coders make during decision-making:

- Performance errors: misreading words, missing details important to the code assignment, failing to pull together details from various parts of the record, transposing digits in code numbers.

- Systematic errors: lack of sufficient medical knowledge to understand the documentation, lack of knowledge of or misapplication of coding rules.[2]

Although coding without physician documentation flies in the face of compliance guidance, offices and facilities in a hurry to keep their cash flow moving will code with only parts of the record complete. For example, a pathology report with the ultimate diagnosis for a surgical specimen may not be available for a week after the surgery. If the patient has been discharged, the hospital will be interested in getting its bill out right away. Coding may be based on the surgeon's post-operative diagnosis, and if the surgeon is wrong, the diagnosis could be something different once the pathology report is available. In the CPT realm, the coding of excision of skin lesions depends on whether or not the lesion is cancerous, so coding before the pathology report is available could lead to inaccurate codes and inappropriate reimbursement.

Coders rely heavily on reports that are transcribed from the physician's dictation. If errors are made in transcription, they can also result in incorrect coding.

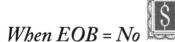

When EOB = No

Your first inkling that your insurance is denying or rejecting a claim for your treatment is usually when you receive an Explanation of Benefits (EOB) from your payer. It tells you what was billed, what has been approved, what has been paid, and what you have to pay. If a claim or part of a claim was rejected, the EOB will use a reason code to tell you why. The problem with the reason codes is that they are not always specific enough to identify the actual problem. Here is an example "Claim lacks information needed for adjudication." You are shaking your head and asking "what information?"

As you investigate the cause of the rejection and work to obtain payment for the claim, it is essential that you maintain a record of your contacts and correspondence:

- Set up a file folder for each provider. If you don't have file folders, even just a folded piece of paper with the provider's name on the outside can help keep your documents in order.

- Make sure you keep all of the EOBs, even if it does not indicate a rejection. They can be useful if you are later involved in a dispute about the bill for service.

- When you receive bills from providers, put them in the appropriate folder, by date. If you pay the bill in person or send a check, keep any receipts or cancelled checks or credit card statements attached to the corresponding bill.

- When you are involved in discussions with provider business offices or insurance company customer service centers, make a note of the date and time of your call, and the specific name of the individual with whom you speak.

- Keep copies of letters or other correspondence you send to providers or insurers.

All of these materials may be needed in backing up future appeals if your initial efforts are not successful.

 Contact the Provider

As a first step after receiving a rejection or denial, it is advisable to contact the healthcare provider who submitted the claim. Sometimes you will receive your EOB before the provider gets their remittance advice, so it is possible they may not be aware of your problem.

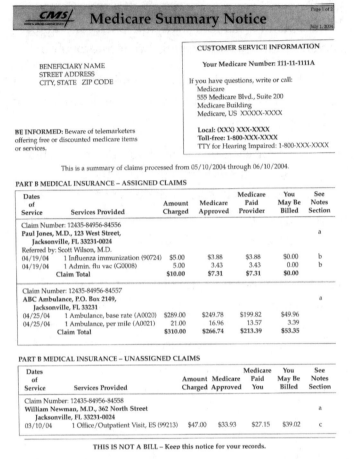

Figure 6-1   Medicare EOB

The provider's business office should be able to help you analyze the rejection and let you know whether they plan to appeal. Their staff may be better at figuring out why the claim was rejected than you, so it is worth a phone call.

Inconsistencies and omissions are obvious provider errors in claims submissions. Some of the coding-related rejection reasons the provider should be able to fix and re-submit are:

- Missing data elements, such as diagnosis code, procedure code, date of service

- Incorrect data elements, such as diagnosis or procedure codes not valid on the date of service (remember that all coding systems change at least annually)

- Inconsistent data elements such as diagnosis or procedure codes that do not match with your gender or age. It is also possible for a procedure code to be inconsistent with the place of service, such as an inpatient code used in a doctor's office

- Incorrectly used data elements, such as modifiers that do not go with the type of procedure code used

- Requested documentation not sent; the provider must send copies of your medical record when requested, for review and approval

Ask for an itemized bill for the episode of care containing denied services.

 Contact the Insurer or other Third-Party Payer

If the rejection is for a reason other than a provider error, contact the insurer to discuss the reason for the rejection.

Rejections of this type are:

- Coverage issues. Procedures can be non-covered for a variety of reasons. It can be due to the specific plan you have, due to the place where the service was provided, or due to the type of provider giving the service. Routine or screening examinations and preventive services are often not covered. The procedure code for the denied service and the diagnosis should be verified.

- Medical necessity. Insurance companies pay for procedures and tests that are intended to improve your condition. They do not cover cosmetic procedures or experimental procedures and may have defined lists of diagnoses for which various procedures are indicated. If your doctor uses a diagnosis not on the list, the claim will not be paid. This can be a coding problem because the documented diagnosis may not have been coded to the appropriate level of specificity, thus causing the denial.

- Frequency limits. Some services are only covered up to a limited number of times within a specified time period. Rejections of this type can be coding problems if an error has been made, for example, in coding the number of chest x-rays you had on a given date.

In interactions with insurance companies, it is important to use the term "appeal." If you use the term "complaint," there may not be an associated time limit within which the company is required to respond. However, with an appeal, a legally-mandated time frame is usually present.

 Request an Internal Review

If you are not satisfied with the results communicated to you by your payer, you may request an internal review. This process varies from payer to payer. You will usually have to complete a formal appeal form and submit it. There may be a time limit for appeals, so make sure you find out how soon you are required to appeal. Employer-sponsored health plans are required to allow you at least 180 days to appeal.

At this point, it may also be helpful to involve others in your efforts. The Human Resources department of your employer may be able to assist you in negotiating with the payer. Your employer contracts with the payer to provide coverage, so your employer has a vested interest in making sure its employees are receiving appropriate coverage and service. If you are a senior citizen, every state has a Senior Health Insurance Assistance Program to help people with insurance problems.

 Request an External Review

Once you have exhausted the internal review process of your payer, in most states you can request an external review. There are often rules about what type of issue can be appealed. Medical necessity cases are the norm. It may also be a requirement that the amount of money in question meet a certain threshold, such as $100 or $500. A helpful website containing information about insurance appeals and various state regulations is the Kaiser Family Foundation at www.kff.org/consumerguide.

 Contact Provider Again

If all else fails, contact the provider once again and explain your situation. Ask if they would consider lowering the price of the denied procedure, service, supply, or drug so that you will have to pay less out of pocket.

References

[1]MIB Group, Inc. Website. Available at http://mib.com/htlm/about_us.html. Accessed October 16, 2004.

[2]Morris WC. Assessing the Accuracy of an Automated Coding System in Emergency Medicine. Available at: http://www.alifemedical.com/documents/LifeCodeEMPerformanceAMIA2000.pdf. Accessed October 16, 2004.

CHAPTER 7

Coding as a Career

Is it Right for You?

Now that you have all the details about medical coding, what it is, and how it works, you may be wondering about a career in this field.

According to the United States Department of Labor, Bureau of Labor Statistics (BLS), job prospects for medical records and health information technicians will grow much faster than average through 2012.[1] About 147,000 individuals are already employed in this field, with about 37% working for hospitals.

This is one of the few health occupations in which there is little or no patient contact.

Average salaries for coders vary by geographic region, size of facility, and type of employer. Entry-level positions are in the $25,000 to $30,000 range. Individuals who are experienced, specialized, or supervisors can make as much as $45,000 to $50,000 or more. Working conditions are generally good, in standard office settings.

Do these attributes describe you?

- Excellent problem-solving skills
- Detail oriented

- Excellent reading comprehension
- Ability to work independently
- Good written / verbal communication skills
- Enthusiasm for learning
- Computer literate
- Ability to multi-task
- Team player

If you enjoy solving puzzles or reading mysteries, coding is just the thing. Every record you review will be different. Every doctor has different methods of documenting care. New vocabulary appears in response to changing technology. Codes change annually and the rules change periodically as well. Coding is never the "same old same old."

Where to Start?

Employers who are hiring coders will be looking for either experience or certification. Although it is possible to start out in a clerical position and work your way up to being a coder, those opportunities are not plentiful. It is not necessary to have a college degree to get a job as a coder, but certification helps.

Two national organizations grant credentials to coders:

- The American Health Information Management Association (AHIMA) grants the Certified Coding Associate (CCA), Certified Coding Specialist (CCS), and Certified Coding Specialist—Physician (CCS-P) credentials. All are based on successful completion of a national exam. All exams require a high school diploma or equivalent and although not required, substantial coding experience is recommended. Additional information from AHIMA is available at: http://www.ahima.org.
- The American Academy of Professional Coders (AAPC) grants the Certified Professional Coder (CPC) and Certi-

fied Professional Coder—Hospital (CPC-H) credentials. These are also based on a national exam. Candidates must have two years full-time coding experience. Those without experience may complete the exam but will be designated as apprentices until the required time period is fulfilled.

Additional information from AAPC is available at: http://aapc.com.

A prerequisite for any type of coding certification or study is a thorough knowledge of medical terminology, disease processes, and anatomy and physiology. Courses in these subjects are available at community colleges and trade schools in every state. Many colleges also offer distance learning programs in which classes can be completed at home.

Reference

[1]U.S. Department of Labor, Bureau of Labor Statistics. Occupational Outlook Handbook, 2004-05. Available at: http://www.bls.gov/oco/ocos103.htm. Accessed October 17, 2004.

ICD-9-CM 3-Digit Diagnosis Categories

Note: All valid ICD-9-CM diagnosis codes have 3, 4, or 5 digits. Each diagnosis falls under one of the 3-digit categories listed below. If a 3-digit category is subdivided into codes with 4 or 5 digits, the subdivisions must be used, not the 3-digit category. An example is Cholera, category 001. It is further subdivided into 001.0, 001.2, and 001.9 for different causes of cholera and also cholera, unspecified. The 4-digit codes must be used. The 3-digit category code is not valid.

1. INFECTIOUS AND PARASITIC DISEASES

001	Cholera
002	Typhoid and paratyphoid fevers
003	Other salmonella infections
004	Shigellosis
005	Other food poisoning (bacterial)
006	Amebiasis
007	Other protozoal intestinal diseases
008	Intestinal infections due to other organisms
009	Ill-defined intestinal infections
010	Primary tuberculous infection
011	Pulmonary tuberculosis
012	Other respiratory tuberculosis

013	Tuberculosis of meninges and central nervous system
014	Tuberculosis of intestines, peritoneum, and mesenteric glands
015	Tuberculosis of bones and joints
016	Tuberculosis of genitourinary system
017	Tuberculosis of other organs
018	Miliary tuberculosis
020	Plague
021	Tularemia
022	Anthrax
023	Brucellosis
024	Glanders
025	Melioidosis
026	Rat-bite fever
027	Other zoonotic bacterial diseases
030	Leprosy
031	Diseases due to other mycobacteria
032	Diphtheria
033	Whooping cough
034	Streptococcal sore throat and scarlet fever
035	Erysipelas
036	Meningococcal infection
037	Tetanus
038	Septicemia
039	Actinomycotic infections
040	Other bacterial diseases
041	Bacterial infection in conditions classified elsewhere and of unspecified site
042	Human immunodeficiency virus [HIV] disease
045	Acute poliomyelitis
046	Slow virus infection of central nervous system
047	Meningitis due to enterovirus
048	Other enterovirus diseases of central nervous system
049	Other non-arthropod-borne viral diseases of central nervous system
050	Smallpox
051	Cowpox and paravaccinia
052	Chickenpox
053	Herpes zoster
054	Herpes simplex
055	Measles
056	Rubella
057	Other viral exanthemata
060	Yellow fever

061	Dengue
062	Mosquito-borne viral encephalitis
063	Tick-borne viral encephalitis
064	Viral encephalitis transmitted by other and unspecified arthropods
065	Arthropod-borne hemorrhagic fever
066	Other arthropod-borne viral diseases
070	Viral hepatitis
071	Rabies
072	Mumps
073	Ornithosis
074	Specific diseases due to Coxsackie virus
075	Infectious mononucleosis
076	Trachoma
077	Other diseases of conjunctiva due to viruses and Chlamydiae
078	Other diseases due to viruses and Chlamydiae
079	Viral infection in conditions classified elsewhere and of unspecified site
080	Louse-borne [epidemic] typhus
081	Other typhus
082	Tick-borne rickettsioses
083	Other rickettsioses
084	Malaria
085	Leishmaniasis
086	Trypanosomiasis
087	Relapsing fever
088	Other arthropod-borne diseases
090	Congenital syphilis
091	Early syphilis, symptomatic
092	Early syphilis, latent
093	Cardiovascular syphilis
094	Neurosyphilis
095	Other forms of late syphilis, with symptoms
096	Late syphilis, latent
097	Other and unspecified syphilis
098	Gonococcal infections
099	Other venereal diseases
100	Leptospirosis
101	Vincent's angina
102	Yaws
103	Pinta
104	Other spirochetal infection
110	Dermatophytosis

111	Dermatomycosis, other and unspecified
112	Candidiasis
114	Coccidioidomycosis
115	Histoplasmosis
116	Blastomycotic infection
117	Other mycoses
118	Opportunistic mycoses
120	Schistosomiasis [bilharziasis]
121	Other trematode infections
122	Echinococcosis
123	Other cestode infection
124	Trichinosis
125	Filarial infection and dracontiasis
126	Ancylostomiasis and necatoriasis
127	Other intestinal helminthiases
128	Other and unspecified helminthiases
129	Intestinal parasitism, unspecified
130	Toxoplasmosis
131	Trichomoniasis
132	Pediculosis and phthirus infestation
133	Acariasis
134	Other infestation
135	Sarcoidosis
136	Other and unspecified infectious and parasitic diseases
137	Late effects of tuberculosis
138	Late effects of acute poliomyelitis
139	Late effects of other infectious and parasitic diseases

2. NEOPLASMS

140	Malignant neoplasm of lip
141	Malignant neoplasm of tongue
142	Malignant neoplasm of major salivary glands
143	Malignant neoplasm of gum
144	Malignant neoplasm of floor of mouth
145	Malignant neoplasm of other and unspecified parts of mouth
146	Malignant neoplasm of oropharynx
147	Malignant neoplasm of nasopharynx
148	Malignant neoplasm of hypopharynx
149	Malignant neoplasm of other and ill-defined sites within the lip, oral cavity, and pharynx
150	Malignant neoplasm of esophagus

151   Malignant neoplasm of stomach

152   Malignant neoplasm of small intestine, including duodenum

153   Malignant neoplasm of colon

154   Malignant neoplasm of rectum, rectosigmoid junction, and anus

155   Malignant neoplasm of liver and intrahepatic bile ducts

156   Malignant neoplasm of gallbladder and extrahepatic bile ducts

157   Malignant neoplasm of pancreas

158   Malignant neoplasm of retroperitoneum and peritoneum

159   Malignant neoplasm of other and ill-defined sites within the digestive organs and peritoneum

160   Malignant neoplasm of nasal cavities, middle ear, and accessory sinuses

161   Malignant neoplasm of larynx

162   Malignant neoplasm of trachea, bronchus, and lung

163   Malignant neoplasm of pleura

164   Malignant neoplasm of thymus, heart, and mediastinum

165   Malignant neoplasm of other and ill-defined sites within the respiratory system and intrathoracic organs

170   Malignant neoplasm of bone and articular cartilage

171   Malignant neoplasm of connective and other soft tissue

172   Malignant melanoma of skin

173   Other malignant neoplasm of skin

174   Malignant neoplasm of female breast

175   Malignant neoplasm of male breast

176   Kaposi's sarcoma

179   Malignant neoplasm of uterus, part unspecified

180   Malignant neoplasm of cervix uteri

181   Malignant neoplasm of placenta

182   Malignant neoplasm of body of uterus

183   Malignant neoplasm of ovary and other uterine adnexa

184   Malignant neoplasm of other and unspecified female genital organs

185   Malignant neoplasm of prostate

186   Malignant neoplasm of testis

187   Malignant neoplasm of penis and other male genital organs

188   Malignant neoplasm of bladder

189   Malignant neoplasm of kidney and other and unspecified urinary organs

190   Malignant neoplasm of eye

191   Malignant neoplasm of brain

192   Malignant neoplasm of other and unspecified parts of nervous system

193   Malignant neoplasm of thyroid gland

194   Malignant neoplasm of other endocrine glands and related structures

195   Malignant neoplasm of other and ill-defined sites

196   Secondary and unspecified malignant neoplasm of lymph nodes

197	Secondary malignant neoplasm of respiratory and digestive systems
198	Secondary malignant neoplasm of other specified sites
199	Malignant neoplasm without specification of site
200	Lymphosarcoma and reticulosarcoma
201	Hodgkin's disease
202	Other malignant neoplasm of lymphoid and histiocytic tissue
203	Multiple myeloma and immunoproliferative neoplasms
204	Lymphoid leukemia
205	Myeloid leukemia
206	Monocytic leukemia
207	Other specified leukemia
208	Leukemia of unspecified cell type
210	Benign neoplasm of lip, oral cavity, and pharynx
211	Benign neoplasm of other parts of digestive system
212	Benign neoplasm of respiratory and intrathoracic organs
213	Benign neoplasm of bone and articular cartilage
214	Lipoma
215	Other benign neoplasm of connective and other soft tissue
216	Benign neoplasm of skin
217	Benign neoplasm of breast
218	Uterine leiomyoma
219	Other benign neoplasm of uterus
220	Benign neoplasm of ovary
221	Benign neoplasm of other female genital organs
222	Benign neoplasm of male genital organs
223	Benign neoplasm of kidney and other urinary organs
224	Benign neoplasm of eye
225	Benign neoplasm of brain and other parts of nervous system
226	Benign neoplasm of thyroid gland
227	Benign neoplasm of other endocrine glands and related structures
228	Hemangioma and lymphangioma, any site
229	Benign neoplasm of other and unspecified sites
230	Carcinoma in situ of digestive organs
231	Carcinoma in situ of respiratory system
232	Carcinoma in situ of skin
233	Carcinoma in situ of breast and genitourinary system
234	Carcinoma in situ of other and unspecified sites
235	Neoplasm of uncertain behavior of digestive and respiratory systems
236	Neoplasm of uncertain behavior of genitourinary organs
237	Neoplasm of uncertain behavior of endocrine glands and nervous system
238	Neoplasm of uncertain behavior of other and unspecified sites and tissues

239   Neoplasm of unspecified nature

3. ENDOCRINE, NUTRITIONAL AND METABOLIC DISEASES, AND IMMUNITY DISORDERS

240   Simple and unspecified goiter

241   Nontoxic nodular goiter

242   Thyrotoxicosis with or without goiter

243   Congenital hypothyroidism

244   Acquired hypothyroidism

245   Thyroiditis

246   Other disorders of thyroid

250   Diabetes mellitus

251   Other disorders of pancreatic internal secretion

252   Disorders of parathyroid gland

253   Disorders of the pituitary gland and its hypothalamic control

254   Diseases of thymus gland

255   Disorders of adrenal glands

256   Ovarian dysfunction

257   Testicular dysfunction

258   Polyglandular dysfunction and related disorders

259   Other endocrine disorders

260   Kwashiorkor

261   Nutritional marasmus

262   Other severe protein-calorie malnutrition

263   Other and unspecified protein-calorie malnutrition

264   Vitamin A deficiency

265   Thiamine and niacin deficiency states

266   Deficiency of B-complex components

267   Ascorbic acid deficiency

268   Vitamin D deficiency

269   Other nutritional deficiencies

270   Disorders of amino-acid transport and metabolism

271   Disorders of carbohydrate transport and metabolism

272   Disorders of lipoid metabolism

273   Disorders of plasma protein metabolism

274   Gout

275   Disorders of mineral metabolism

276   Disorders of fluid, electrolyte, and acid-base balance

277   Other and unspecified disorders of metabolism

278   Obesity and other hyperalimentation

279   Disorders involving the immune mechanism

4. DISEASES OF THE BLOOD AND BLOOD-FORMING ORGANS

280   Iron deficiency anemias
281   Other deficiency anemias
282   Hereditary hemolytic anemias
283   Acquired hemolytic anemias
284   Aplastic anemia
285   Other and unspecified anemias
286   Coagulation defects
287   Purpura and other hemorrhagic conditions
288   Diseases of white blood cells
289   Other diseases of blood and blood-forming organs

5. MENTAL DISORDERS

290   Senile and presenile organic psychotic conditions
291   Alcoholic psychoses
292   Drug psychoses
293   Transient organic psychotic conditions
294   Other organic psychotic conditions (chronic)
295   Schizophrenic psychoses
296   Affective psychoses
297   Paranoid states
298   Other nonorganic psychoses
299   Psychoses with origin specific to childhood
300   Neurotic disorders
301   Personality disorders
302   Sexual deviations and disorders
303   Alcohol dependence syndrome
304   Drug dependence
305   Nondependent abuse of drugs
306   Physiological malfunction arising from mental factors
307   Special symptoms or syndromes, not elsewhere classified
308   Acute reaction to stress
309   Adjustment reaction
310   Specific nonpsychotic mental disorders following organic brain damage
311   Depressive disorder, not elsewhere classified
312   Disturbance of conduct, not elsewhere classified
313   Disturbance of emotions specific to childhood and adolescence
314   Hyperkinetic syndrome of childhood
315   Specific delays in development

316 Psychic factors associated with diseases classified elsewhere

317 Mild mental retardation

318 Other specified mental retardation

319 Unspecified mental retardation

6. DISEASES OF THE NERVOUS SYSTEM AND SENSE ORGANS

320 Bacterial meningitis

321 Meningitis due to other organisms

322 Meningitis of unspecified cause

323 Encephalitis, myelitis, and encephalomyelitis

324 Intracranial and intraspinal abscess

325 Phlebitis and thrombophlebitis of intracranial venous sinuses

326 Late effects of intracranial abscess or pyogenic infection

330 Cerebral degenerations usually manifest in childhood

331 Other cerebral degenerations

332 Parkinson's disease

333 Other extrapyramidal disease and abnormal movement disorders

334 Spinocerebellar disease

335 Anterior horn cell disease

336 Other diseases of spinal cord

337 Disorders of the autonomic nervous system

340 Multiple sclerosis

341 Other demyelinating diseases of central nervous system

342 Hemiplegia and hemiparesis

343 Infantile cerebral palsy

344 Other paralytic syndromes

345 Epilepsy

346 Migraine

347 Cataplexy and narcolepsy

348 Other conditions of brain

349 Other and unspecified disorders of the nervous system

350 Trigeminal nerve disorders

351 Facial nerve disorders

352 Disorders of other cranial nerves

353 Nerve root and plexus disorders

354 Mononeuritis of upper limb and mononeuritis multiplex

355 Mononeuritis of lower limb

356 Hereditary and idiopathic peripheral neuropathy

357 Inflammatory and toxic neuropathy

358 Myoneural disorders

359   Muscular dystrophies and other myopathies
360   Disorders of the globe
361   Retinal detachments and defects
362   Other retinal disorders
363   Chorioretinal inflammations and scars and other disorders of choroid
364   Disorders of iris and ciliary body
365   Glaucoma
366   Cataract
367   Disorders of refraction and accommodation
368   Visual disturbances
369   Blindness and low vision
370   Keratitis
371   Corneal opacity and other disorders of cornea
372   Disorders of conjunctiva
373   Inflammation of eyelids
374   Other disorders of eyelids
375   Disorders of lacrimal system
376   Disorders of the orbit
377   Disorders of optic nerve and visual pathways
378   Strabismus and other disorders of binocular eye movements
379   Other disorders of eye
380   Disorders of external ear
381   Nonsuppurative otitis media and Eustachian tube disorders
382   Suppurative and unspecified otitis media
383   Mastoiditis and related conditions
384   Other disorders of tympanic membrane
385   Other disorders of middle ear and mastoid
386   Vertiginous syndromes and other disorders of vestibular system
387   Otosclerosis
388   Other disorders of ear
389   Hearing loss

7. DISEASES OF THE CIRCULATORY SYSTEM

390   Rheumatic fever without mention of heart involvement
391   Rheumatic fever with heart involvement
392   Rheumatic chorea
393   Chronic rheumatic pericarditis
394   Diseases of mitral valve
395   Diseases of aortic valve
396   Diseases of mitral and aortic valves

397	Diseases of other endocardial structures
398	Other rheumatic heart disease
401	Essential hypertension
402	Hypertensive heart disease
403	Hypertensive renal disease
404	Hypertensive heart and renal disease
405	Secondary hypertension
410	Acute myocardial infarction
411	Other acute and subacute form of ischemic heart disease
412	Old myocardial infarction
413	Angina pectoris
414	Other forms of chronic ischemic heart disease
415	Acute pulmonary heart disease
416	Chronic pulmonary heart disease
417	Other diseases of pulmonary circulation
420	Acute pericarditis
421	Acute and subacute endocarditis
422	Acute myocarditis
423	Other diseases of pericardium
424	Other diseases of endocardium
425	Cardiomyopathy
426	Conduction disorders
427	Cardiac dysrhythmias
428	Heart failure
429	Ill-defined descriptions and complications of heart disease
430	Subarachnoid hemorrhage
431	Intracerebral hemorrhage
432	Other and unspecified intracranial hemorrhage
433	Occlusion and stenosis of precerebral arteries
434	Occlusion of cerebral arteries
435	Transcient cerebral ischemia
436	Acute but ill-defined cerebrovascular disease
437	Other and ill-defined cerebrovascular disease
438	Late effects of cerebrovascular disease
440	Atherosclerosis
441	Aortic aneurysm and dissection
442	Other aneurysm
443	Other peripheral vascular disease
444	Arterial embolism and thrombosis
445	Atheroembolism
446	Polyarteritis nodosa and allied conditions

447   Other disorders of arteries and arterioles

448   Diseases of capillaries

451   Phlebitis and thrombophlebitis

452   Portal vein thrombosis

453   Other venous embolism and thrombosis

454   Varicose veins of lower extremities

455   Hemorrhoids

456   Varicose veins of other sites

457   Noninfective disorders of lymphatic channels

458   Hypotension

459   Other disorders of circulatory system

8. DISEASES OF THE RESPIRATORY SYSTEM

460   Acute nasopharyngitis [common cold]

461   Acute sinusitis

462   Acute pharyngitis

463   Acute tonsillitis

464   Acute laryngitis and tracheitis

465   Acute upper respiratory infections of multiple or unspecified sites

466   Acute bronchitis and bronchiolitis

470   Deviated nasal septum

471   Nasal polyps

472   Chronic pharyngitis and nasopharyngitis

473   Chronic sinusitis

474   Chronic disease of tonsils and adenoids

475   Peritonsillar abscess

476   Chronic laryngitis and laryngotracheitis

477   Allergic rhinitis

478   Other diseases of upper respiratory tract

480   Viral pneumonia

481   Pneumococcal pneumonia [Streptococcus pneumoniae pneumonia]

482   Other bacterial pneumonia

483   Pneumonia due to other specified organism

484   Pneumonia in infectious diseases classified elsewhere

485   Bronchopneumonia, organism unspecified

486   Pneumonia, organism unspecified

487   Influenza

490   Bronchitis, not specified as acute or chronic

491   Chronic bronchitis

492   Emphysema

493   Asthma

494   Bronchiectasis

495   Extrinsic allergic alveolitis

496   Chronic airways obstruction, not elsewhere classified

500   Coalworkers' pneumoconiosis

501   Asbestosis

502   Pneumoconiosis due to other silica or silicates

503   Pneumoconiosis due to other inorganic dust

504   Pneumopathy due to inhalation of other dust

505   Pneumoconiosis, unspecified

506   Respiratory conditions due to chemical fumes and vapors

507   Pneumonitis due to solids and liquids

508   Respiratory conditions due to other and unspecified external agents

510   Empyema

511   Pleurisy

512   Pneumothorax

513   Abscess of lung and mediastinum

514   Pulmonary congestion and hypostasis

515   Postinflammatory pulmonary fibrosis

516   Other alveolar and parietoalveolar pneumopathy

517   Lung involvement in conditions classified elsewhere

518   Other diseases of lung

519   Other diseases of respiratory system

9. DISEASES OF THE DIGESTIVE SYSTEM

520   Disorders of tooth development and eruption

521   Diseases of hard tissues of teeth

522   Diseases of pulp and periapical tissues

523   Gingival and periodontal diseases

524   Dentofacial anomalies, including malocclusion

525   Other diseases and conditions of the teeth and supporting structures

526   Diseases of the jaws

527   Diseases of the salivary glands

528   Diseases of the oral soft tissues, excluding lesions specific for gingiva and tongue

529   Diseases and other conditions of the tongue

530   Diseases of esophagus

531   Gastric ulcer

532   Duodenal ulcer

533   Peptic ulcer, site unspecified

534   Gastrojejunal ulcer

535 Gastritis and duodenitis

536 Disorders of function of stomach

537 Other disorders of stomach and duodenum

540 Acute appendicitis

541 Appendicitis, unqualified

542 Other appendicitis

543 Other diseases of appendix

550 Inguinal hernia

551 Other hernia of abdominal cavity, with gangrene

552 Other hernia of abdominal cavity, with obstruction, but without mention of gangrene

553 Other hernia of abdominal cavity without mention of obstruction or gangrene

555 Regional enteritis

556 Ulcerative colitis

557 Vascular insufficiency of intestine

558 Other noninfective gastroenteritis and colitis

560 Intestinal obstruction without mention of hernia

562 Diverticula of intestine

564 Functional digestive disorders, not elsewhere classified

565 Anal fissure and fistula

566 Abscess of anal and rectal regions

567 Peritonitis

568 Other disorders of peritoneum

569 Other disorders of intestine

570 Acute and subacute necrosis of liver

571 Chronic liver disease and cirrhosis

572 Liver abscess and sequelae of chronic liver disease

573 Other disorders of liver

574 Cholelithiasis

575 Other disorders of gallbladder

576 Other disorders of biliary tract

577 Diseases of pancreas

578 Gastrointestinal hemorrhage

579 Intestinal malabsorption

10. DISEASES OF THE GENITOURINARY SYSTEM

580 Acute glomerulonephritis

581 Nephrotic syndrome

582 Chronic glomerulonephritis

583 Nephritis and nephropathy, not specified as acute or chronic

584 Acute renal failure

585	Chronic renal failure
586	Renal failure, unspecified
587	Renal sclerosis, unspecified
588	Disorders resulting from impaired renal function
589	Small kidney of unknown cause
590	Infections of kidney
591	Hydronephrosis
592	Calculus of kidney and ureter
593	Other disorders of kidney and ureter
594	Calculus of lower urinary tract
595	Cystitis
596	Other disorders of bladder
597	Urethritis, not sexually transmitted, and urethral syndrome
598	Urethral stricture
599	Other disorders of urethra and urinary tract
600	Hyperplasia of prostate
601	Inflammatory diseases of prostate
602	Other disorders of prostate
603	Hydrocele
604	Orchitis and epididymitis
605	Redundant prepuce and phimosis
606	Infertility, male
607	Disorders of penis
608	Other disorders of male genital organs
610	Benign mammary dysplasias
611	Other disorders of breast
614	Inflammatory disease of ovary, fallopian tube, pelvic cellular tissue, and peritoneum
615	Inflammatory diseases of uterus, except cervix
616	Inflammatory disease of cervix, vagina, and vulva
617	Endometriosis
618	Genital prolapse
619	Fistula involving female genital tract
620	Noninflammatory disorders of ovary, fallopian tube, and broad ligament
621	Disorders of uterus, not elsewhere classified
622	Noninflammatory disorders of cervix
623	Noninflammatory disorders of vagina
624	Noninflammatory disorders of vulva and perineum
625	Pain and other symptoms associated with female genital organs
626	Disorders of menstruation and other abnormal bleeding from female genital tract
627	Menopausal and postmenopausal disorders

628   Infertility, female

629   Other disorders of female genital organs

11. COMPLICATIONS OF PREGNANCY, CHILDBIRTH, AND THE PUERPERIUM

630   Hydatidiform mole

631   Other abnormal product of conception

632   Missed abortion

633   Ectopic pregnancy

634   Spontaneous abortion

635   Legally induced abortion

636   Illegally induced abortion

637   Unspecified abortion

638   Failed attempted abortion

639   Complications following abortion and ectopic and molar pregnancies

640   Hemorrhage in early pregnancy

641   Antepartum hemorrhage, abruptio placentae, and placenta previa

642   Hypertension complicating pregnancy, childbirth, and the puerperium

643   Excessive vomiting in pregnancy

644   Early or threatened labor

645   Prolonged pregnancy

646   Other complications of pregnancy, not elsewhere classified

647   Infective and parasitic conditions in the mother classifiable elsewhere but complicating pregnancy, childbirth, and the puerperium

648   Other current conditions in the mother classifiable elsewhere but complicating pregnancy, childbirth, and the puerperium

650   Normal delivery

651   Multiple gestation

652   Malposition and malpresentation of fetus

653   Disproportion

654   Abnormality of organs and soft tissues of pelvis

655   Known or suspected fetal abnormality affecting management of mother

656   Other fetal and placental problems affecting management of mother

657   Polyhydramnios

658   Other problems associated with amniotic cavity and membranes

659   Other indications for care or intervention related to labor and delivery and not elsewhere classified

660   Obstructed labor

661   Abnormality of forces of labor

662   Long labor

663   Umbilical cord complications

664   Trauma to perineum and vulva during delivery

665   Other obstetrical trauma

666   Postpartum hemorrhage

667   Retained placenta or membranes, without hemorrhage

668   Complications of the administration of anesthetic or other sedation in labor and delivery

669   Other complications of labor and delivery, not elsewhere classified

670   Major puerperal infection

671   Venous complications in pregnancy and the puerperium

672   Pyrexia of unknown origin during the puerperium

673   Obstetrical pulmonary embolism

674   Other and unspecified complications of the puerperium, not elsewhere classified

675   Infections of the breast and nipple associated with childbirth

676   Other disorders of the breast associated with childbirth, and disorders of lactation

677   Late effect of complication of pregnancy, childbirth, and the puerperium

12. DISEASES OF THE SKIN AND SUBCUTANEOUS TISSUE

680   Carbuncle and furuncle

681   Cellulitis and abscess of finger and toe

682   Other cellulitis and abscess

683   Acute lymphadenitis

684   Impetigo

685   Pilonidal cyst

686   Other local infections of skin and subcutaneous tissue

690   Erythematosquamous dermatosis

691   Atopic dermatitis and related conditions

692   Contact dermatitis and other eczema

693   Dermatitis due to substances taken internally

694   Bullous dermatoses

695   Erythematous conditions

696   Psoriasis and similar disorders

697   Lichen

698   Pruritus and related conditions

700   Corns and callosities

701   Other hypertrophic and atrophic conditions of skin

702   Other dermatoses

703   Diseases of nail

704   Diseases of hair and hair follicles

705   Disorders of sweat glands

706   Diseases of sebaceous glands

707   Chronic ulcer of skin

708   Urticaria

709   Other disorders of skin and subcutaneous tissue

13. DISEASES OF THE MUSCULOSKELETAL SYSTEM AND CONNECTIVE TISSUE

710   Diffuse diseases of connective tissue

711   Arthropathy associated with infections

712   Crystal arthropathies

713   Arthropathy associated with other disorders classified elsewhere

714   Rheumatoid arthritis and other inflammatory polyarthropathies

715   Osteoarthrosis and allied disorders

716   Other and unspecified arthropathies

717   Internal derangement of knee

718   Other derangement of joint

719   Other and unspecified disorder of joint

720   Ankylosing spondylitis and other inflammatory spondylopathies

721   Spondylosis and allied disorders

722   Intervertebral disc disorders

723   Other disorders of cervical region

724   Other and unspecified disorders of back

725   Polymyalgia rheumatica

726   Peripheral enthesopathies and allied syndromes

727   Other disorders of synovium, tendon, and bursa

728   Disorders of muscle, ligament, and fascia

729   Other disorders of soft tissues

730   Osteomyelitis, periostitis, and other infections involving bone

731   Osteitis deformans and osteopathies associated with other disorders classified elsewhere

732   Osteochondropathies

733   Other disorders of bone and cartilage

734   Flat foot

735   Acquired deformities of toe

736   Other acquired deformities of limbs

737   Curvature of spine

738   Other acquired deformity

739   Nonallopathic lesions, not elsewhere classified

14. CONGENITAL ANOMALIES

740   Anencephalus and similar anomalies

741   Spina bifida

742   Other congenital anomalies of nervous system

743   Congenital anomalies of eye

744   Congenital anomalies of ear, face, and neck

745   Bulbus cordis anomalies and anomalies of cardiac septal closure

746   Other congenital anomalies of heart

747   Other congenital anomalies of circulatory system

748   Congenital anomalies of respiratory system

749   Cleft palate and cleft lip

750   Other congenital anomalies of upper alimentary tract

751   Other congenital anomalies of digestive system

752   Congenital anomalies of genital organs

753   Congenital anomalies of urinary system

754   Certain congenital musculoskeletal deformities

755   Other congenital anomalies of limbs

756   Other congenital musculoskeletal anomalies

757   Congenital anomalies of the integument

758   Chromosomal anomalies

759   Other and unspecified congenital anomalies

15. CERTAIN CONDITIONS ORIGINATING IN THE PERINATAL PERIOD

760   Fetus or newborn affected by maternal conditions which may be unrelated to present pregnancy

761   Fetus or newborn affected by maternal complications of pregnancy

762   Fetus or newborn affected by complications of placenta, cord, and membranes

763   Fetus or newborn affected by other complications of labor and delivery

764   Slow fetal growth and fetal malnutrition

765   Disorders relating to short gestation and unspecified low birthweight

766   Disorders relating to long gestation and high birthweight

767   Birth trauma

768   Intrauterine hypoxia and birth asphyxia

769   Respiratory distress syndrome

770   Other respiratory conditions of fetus and newborn

771   Infections specific to the perinatal period

772   Fetal and neonatal hemorrhage

773   Hemolytic disease of fetus or newborn, due to isoimmunization

774   Other perinatal jaundice

775   Endocrine and metabolic disturbances specific to the fetus and newborn

776   Hematological disorders of fetus and newborn

777   Perinatal disorders of digestive system

778   Conditions involving the integument and temperature regulation of fetus and newborn

779   Other and ill-defined conditions originating in the perinatal period

16. SYMPTOMS, SIGNS, AND ILL-DEFINED CONDITIONS

780   General symptoms
781   Symptoms involving nervous and musculoskeletal systems
782   Symptoms involving skin and other integumentary tissue
783   Symptoms concerning nutrition, metabolism, and development
784   Symptoms involving head and neck
785   Symptoms involving cardiovascular system
786   Symptoms involving respiratory system and other chest symptoms
787   Symptoms involving digestive system
788   Symptoms involving urinary system
789   Other symptoms involving abdomen and pelvis
790   Nonspecific findings on examination of blood
791   Nonspecific findings on examination of urine
792   Nonspecific abnormal findings in other body substances
793   Nonspecific abnormal findings on radiological and other examination of body structure
794   Nonspecific abnormal results of function studies
795   Nonspecific abnormal histological and immunological findings
796   Other nonspecific abnormal findings
797   Senility without mention of psychosis
798   Sudden death, cause unknown
799   Other ill-defined and unknown causes of morbidity and mortality

17. INJURY AND POISONING

800   Fracture of vault of skull
801   Fracture of base of skull
802   Fracture of face bones
803   Other and unqualified skull fractures
804   Multiple fractures involving skull or face with other bones
805   Fracture of vertebral column without mention of spinal cord lesion
806   Fracture of vertebral column with spinal cord lesion
807   Fracture of rib(s), sternum, larynx, and trachea
808   Fracture of pelvis
809   Ill-defined fractures of bones of trunk
810   Fracture of clavicle
811   Fracture of scapula
812   Fracture of humerus
813   Fracture of radius and ulna
814   Fracture of carpal bone(s)

815	Fracture of metacarpal bone(s)
816	Fracture of one or more phalanges of hand
817	Multiple fractures of hand bones
818	Ill-defined fractures of upper limb
819	Multiple fractures involving both upper limbs, and upper limb with rib(s) and sternum
820	Fracture of neck of femur
821	Fracture of other and unspecified parts of femur
822	Fracture of patella
823	Fracture of tibia and fibula
824	Fracture of ankle
825	Fracture of one or more tarsal and metatarsal bones
826	Fracture of one or more phalanges of foot
827	Other, multiple, and ill-defined fractures of lower limb
828	Multiple fractures involving both lower limbs, lower with upper limb, and lower limb(s) with rib(s) and sternum
829	Fracture of unspecified bones
830	Dislocation of jaw
831	Dislocation of shoulder
832	Dislocation of elbow
833	Dislocation of wrist
834	Dislocation of finger
835	Dislocation of hip
836	Dislocation of knee
837	Dislocation of ankle
838	Dislocation of foot
839	Other, multiple, and ill-defined dislocations
840	Sprains and strains of shoulder and upper arm
841	Sprains and strains of elbow and forearm
842	Sprains and strains of wrist and hand
843	Sprains and strains of hip and thigh
844	Sprains and strains of knee and leg
845	Sprains and strains of ankle and foot
846	Sprains and strains of sacroiliac region
847	Sprains and strains of other and unspecified parts of back
848	Other and ill-defined sprains and strains
850	Concussion
851	Cerebral laceration and contusion
852	Subarachnoid, subdural, and extradural hemorrhage, following injury
853	Other and unspecified intracranial hemorrhage following injury
854	Intracranial injury of other and unspecified nature
860	Traumatic pneumothorax and hemothorax

861	Injury to heart and lung
862	Injury to other and unspecified intrathoracic organs
863	Injury to gastrointestinal tract
864	Injury to liver
865	Injury to spleen
866	Injury to kidney
867	Injury to pelvic organs
868	Injury to other intra-abdominal organs
869	Internal injury to unspecified or ill-defined organs
870	Open wound of ocular adnexa
871	Open wound of eyeball
872	Open wound of ear
873	Other open wound of head
874	Open wound of neck
875	Open wound of chest (wall)
876	Open wound of back
877	Open wound of buttock
878	Open wound of genital organs (external), including traumatic amputation
879	Open wound of other and unspecified sites, except limbs
880	Open wound of shoulder and upper arm
(881)	Open wound of elbow, forearm, and wrist
882	Open wound of hand except finger(s) alone
883	Open wound of finger(s)
884	Multiple and unspecified open wound of upper limb
885	Traumatic amputation of thumb (complete) (partial)
886	Traumatic amputation of other finger(s) (complete) (partial)
887	Traumatic amputation of arm and hand (complete) (partial)
890	Open wound of hip and thigh
891	Open wound of knee, leg [except thigh], and ankle
892	Open wound of foot except toe(s) alone
893	Open wound of toe(s)
894	Multiple and unspecified open wound of lower limb
895	Traumatic amputation of toe(s) (complete) (partial)
896	Traumatic amputation of foot (complete) (partial)
897	Traumatic amputation of leg(s) (complete) (partial)
900	Injury to blood vessels of head and neck
901	Injury to blood vessels of thorax
902	Injury to blood vessels of abdomen and pelvis
903	Injury to blood vessels of upper extremity
904	Injury to blood vessels of lower extremity and unspecified sites
905	Late effects of musculoskeletal and connective tissue injuries

906	Late effects of injuries to skin and subcutaneous tissues
907	Late effects of injuries to the nervous system
908	Late effects of other and unspecified injuries
909	Late effects of other and unspecified external causes
910	Superficial injury of face, neck, and scalp except eye
911	Superficial injury of trunk
912	Superficial injury of shoulder and upper arm
913	Superficial injury of elbow, forearm, and wrist
914	Superficial injury of hand(s) except finger(s) alone
915	Superficial injury of finger(s)
916	Superficial injury of hip, thigh, leg, and ankle
917	Superficial injury of foot and toe(s)
918	Superficial injury of eye and adnexa
919	Superficial injury of other, multiple, and unspecified sites
920	Contusion of face, scalp, and neck except eye(s)
921	Contusion of eye and adnexa
922	Contusion of trunk
923	Contusion of upper limb
924	Contusion of lower limb and of other and unspecified sites
925	Crushing injury of face, scalp, and neck
926	Crushing injury of trunk
927	Crushing injury of upper limb
928	Crushing injury of lower limb
929	Crushing injury of multiple and unspecified sites
930	Foreign body on external eye
931	Foreign body in ear
932	Foreign body in nose
933	Foreign body in pharynx and larynx
934	Foreign body in trachea, bronchus, and lung
935	Foreign body in mouth, esophagus, and stomach
936	Foreign body in intestine and colon
937	Foreign body in anus and rectum
938	Foreign body in digestive system, unspecified
939	Foreign body in genitourinary tract
940	Burn confined to eye and adnexa
941	Burn of face, head, and neck
942	Burn of trunk
943	Burn of upper limb, except wrist and hand
944	Burn of wrist(s) and hand(s)
945	Burn of lower limb(s)
946	Burns of multiple specified sites

947	Burn of internal organs
948	Burns classified according to extent of body surface involved
949	Burn, unspecified
950	Injury to optic nerve and pathways
951	Injury to other cranial nerve(s)
952	Spinal cord injury without evidence of spinal bone injury
953	Injury to nerve roots and spinal plexus
954	Injury to other nerve(s) of trunk excluding shoulder and pelvic girdles
955	Injury to peripheral nerve(s) of shoulder girdle and upper limb
956	Injury to peripheral nerve(s) of pelvic girdle and lower limb
957	Injury to other and unspecified nerves
958	Certain early complications of trauma
959	Injury, other and unspecified
960	Poisoning by antibiotics
961	Poisoning by other anti-infectives
962	Poisoning by hormones and synthetic substitutes
963	Poisoning by primarily systemic agents
964	Poisoning by agents primarily affecting blood constituents
965	Poisoning by analgesics, antipyretics, and antirheumatics
966	Poisoning by anticonvulsants and anti-Parkinsonism drugs
967	Poisoning by sedatives and hypnotics
968	Poisoning by other central nervous system depressants and anesthetics
969	Poisoning by psychotropic agents
970	Poisoning by central nervous system stimulants
971	Poisoning by drugs primarily affecting the autonomic nervous system
972	Poisoning by agents primarily affecting the cardiovascular system
973	Poisoning by agents primarily affecting the gastrointestinal system
974	Poisoning by water, mineral, and uric acid metabolism drugs
975	Poisoning by agents primarily acting on the smooth and skeletal muscles and respiratory system
976	Poisoning by agents primarily affecting skin and mucous membrane, ophthalmological, otorhinolaryngological, and dental drugs
977	Poisoning by other and unspecified drugs and medicinals
978	Poisoning by bacterial vaccines
979	Poisoning by other vaccines and biological substances
980	Toxic effect of alcohol
981	Toxic effect of petroleum products
982	Toxic effect of solvents other than petroleum-based
983	Toxic effect of corrosive aromatics, acids, and caustic alkalis
984	Toxic effect of lead and its compounds (including fumes)
985	Toxic effect of other metals
986	Toxic effect of carbon monoxide

987 Toxic effect of other gases, fumes, or vapors
988 Toxic effect of noxious substances eaten as food
989 Toxic effect of other substances, chiefly nonmedicinal as to source
990 Effects of radiation, unspecified
991 Effects of reduced temperature
992 Effects of heat and light
993 Effects of air pressure
994 Effects of other external causes
995 Certain adverse effects, not elsewhere classified
996 Complications peculiar to certain specified procedures
997 Complications affecting specified body systems, not elsewhere classified
998 Other complications of procedures, not elsewhere classified
999 Complications of medical care, not elsewhere classified

SUPPLEMENTARY CLASSIFICATION OF FACTORS INFLUENCING HEALTH STATUS AND CONTACT WITH HEALTH SERVICES

V01 Contact with or exposure to communicable diseases
V02 Carrier or suspected carrier of infectious diseases
V03 Need for prophylactic vaccination and inoculation against bacterial diseases
V04 Need for prophylactic vaccination and inoculation against certain viral diseases
V05 Need for other prophylactic vaccination and inoculation against single diseases
V06 Need for prophylactic vaccination and inoculation against combinations of diseases
V07 Need for isolation and other prophylactic measures
V08 Asymptomatic human immunodeficiency virus [HIV] infection status
V09 Infection with drug-resistant microorganisms
V10 Personal history of malignant neoplasm
V11 Personal history of mental disorder
V12 Personal history of certain other diseases
V13 Personal history of other diseases
V14 Personal history of allergy to medicinal agents
V15 Other personal history presenting hazards to health
V16 Family history of malignant neoplasm
V17 Family history of certain chronic disabling diseases
V18 Family history of certain other specific conditions
V19 Family history of other conditions
V20 Health supervision of infant or child
V21 Constitutional states in development
V22 Normal pregnancy
V23 Supervision of high-risk pregnancy
V24 Postpartum care and examination

V25	Encounter for contraceptive management
V26	Procreative management
V27	Outcome of delivery
V28	Antenatal screening
V29	Observation and evaluation of newborns and infants for suspected condition not found
V30	Single liveborn
V31	Twin, mate liveborn
V32	Twin, mate stillborn
V33	Twin, unspecified
V34	Other multiple, mates all liveborn
V35	Other multiple, mates all stillborn
V36	Other multiple, mates live- and stillborn
V37	Other multiple, unspecified
V39	Unspecified
V40	Mental and behavioral problems
V41	Problems with special senses and other special functions
V42	Organ or tissue replaced by transplant
V43	Organ or tissue replaced by other means
V44	Artificial opening status
V45	Other postsurgical states
V46	Other dependence on machines
V47	Other problems with internal organs
V48	Problems with head, neck, and trunk
V49	Problems with limbs and other problems
V50	Elective surgery for purposes other than remedying health states
V51	Aftercare involving the use of plastic surgery
V52	Fitting and adjustment of prosthetic device
V53	Fitting and adjustment of other device
V54	Other orthopedic aftercare
V55	Attention to artificial openings
V56	Encounter for dialysis and dialysis catheter care
V57	Care involving use of rehabilitation procedures
V58	Other and unspecified aftercare
V59	Donors
V60	Housing, household, and economic circumstances
V61	Other family circumstances
V62	Other psychosocial circumstances
V63	Unavailability of other medical facilities for care
V64	Persons encountering health services for specific procedures, not carried out
V65	Other persons seeking consultation without complaint or sickness
V66	Convalescence and palliative care

V67	Follow-up examination
V68	Encounters for administrative purposes
V69	Problems related to lifestyle
V70	General medical examination
V71	Observation and evaluation for suspected conditions
V72	Special investigations and examinations
V73	Special screening examination for viral and chlamydial diseases
V74	Special screening examination for bacterial and spirochetal diseases
V75	Special screening examination for other infectious diseases
V76	Special screening for malignant neoplasms
V77	Special screening for endocrine, nutritional, metabolic, and immunity disorders
V78	Special screening for disorders of blood and blood-forming organs
V79	Special screening for mental disorders and developmental handicaps
V80	Special screening for neurological, eye, and ear diseases
V81	Special screening for cardiovascular, respiratory, and genitourinary diseases
V82	Special screening for other conditions
V83	Genetic carrier status

ICD-9-CM 2-Digit Procedure Categories

Note: All valid ICD-9-CM procedure codes have 3 or 4 digits. Each procedure falls under one of the 2-digit categories listed below. If a 2-digit category is subdivided into codes with 3 or 4 digits, the subdivisions must be used, not the 2-digit category.

00	Procedures and interventions, not Elsewhere Classified
01	Incision and excision of skull, brain, and cerebral meninges
02	Other operations on skull, brain, and cerebral meninges
03	Operations on spinal cord and spinal canal structures
04	Operations on cranial and peripheral nerves
05	Operations on sympathetic nerves or ganglia
06	Operations on thyroid and parathyroid glands
07	Operations on other endocrine glands
08	Operations on eyelids
09	Operations on lacrimal system
10	Operations on conjunctiva
11	Operations on cornea
12	Operations on iris, ciliary body, sclera, and anterior chamber
13	Operations on lens
14	Operations on retina, choroid, vitreous, and posterior chamber
15	Operations on extraocular muscles
16	Operations on orbit and eyeball
17	(Not used)
18	Operations on external ear
19	Reconstructive operations on middle ear

20   Other operations on middle and inner ear

21   Operations on nose

22   Operations on nasal sinuses

23   Removal and restoration of teeth

24   Other operations on teeth, gums, and alveoli

25   Operations on tongue

26   Operations on salivary glands and ducts

27   Other operations on mouth and face

28   Operations on tonsils and adenoids

29   Operations on pharynx

30   Excision of larynx

31   Other operations on larynx and trachea

32   Excision of lung and bronchus

33   Other operations on lung and bronchus

34   Operations on chest wall, pleura, mediastinum, and diaphragm

35   Operations on valves and septa of heart

36   Operations on vessels of heart

37   Other operations on heart and pericardium

38   Incision, excision, and occlusion of vessels

39   Other operations on vessels

40   Operations on lymphatic system

41   Operations on bone marrow and spleen

42   Operations on esophagus

43   Incision and excision of stomach

44   Other operations on stomach

45   Incision, excision, and anastomosis of intestine

46   Other operations on intestine

47   Operations on appendix

48   Operations on rectum, rectosigmoid and perirectal tissue

49   Operations on anus

50   Operations on liver

51   Operations on gallbladder and biliary tract

52   Operations on pancreas

53   Repair of hernia

54   Other operations on abdominal region

55   Operations on kidney

56   Operations on ureter

57   Operations on urinary bladder

58   Operations on urethra

59   Other operations on urinary tract

60   Operations on prostate and seminal vesicles

61	Operations on scrotum and tunica vaginalis
62	Operations on testes
63	Operations on spermatic cord, epididymis, and vas deferens
64	Operations on penis
65	Operations on ovary
66	Operations on fallopian tubes
67	Operations on cervix
68	Other incision and excision of uterus
69	Other operations on uterus and supporting structures
70	Operations on vagina and cul-de-sac
71	Operations on vulva and perineum
72	Forceps, vacuum, and breech delivery
73	Other procedures inducing or assisting delivery
74	Cesarean section and removal of fetus
75	Other obstetric operations
76	Operations on facial bones and joints
77	Incision, excision, and division of other bones
78	Other operations on bones, except facial bones
79	Reduction of fracture and dislocation
80	Incision and excision of joint structures
81	Repair and plastic operations on joint structures
82	Operations on muscle, tendon, and fascia of hand
83	Operations on muscle, tendon, fascia, and bursa, except hand
84	Other procedures on musculoskeletal system
85	Operations on the breast
86	Operations on skin and subcutaneous tissue
87	Diagnostic Radiology
88	Other diagnostic radiology and related techniques
89	Interview, evaluation, consultation, and examination
90	Microscopic examination-I
91	Microscopic examination-II
92	Nuclear medicine
93	Physical therapy, respiratory therapy, rehabilitation, and related procedures
94	Procedures related to the psyche
95	Ophthalmologic and otologic diagnosis and treatment
96	Nonoperative intubation and irrigation
97	Replacement and removal of therapeutic appliances
98	Nonoperative removal of foreign body or calculus
99	Other nonoperative procedures

American Health Information Management Association

Code of Ethics 2004

The following ethical principles are based on the core values of the American Health Information Management Association and apply to all health information management professionals. Guidelines included for each ethical principle are a non-inclusive list of behaviors and situations that can help to clarify the principle. They are not to be meant as a comprehensive list of all situations that can occur.

I. **Advocate, uphold, and defend the individual's right to privacy and the doctrine of confidentiality in the use and disclosure of information.**

Health information management professionals shall:

1.1. Protect all confidential information to include personal, health, financial, genetic, and outcome information.

1.2. Engage in social and political action that supports the protection of privacy and confidentiality, and be aware of the impact of the political arena on the health information system. Advocate for changes in policy and legislation to ensure protection of privacy and confidentiality, coding compliance, and other issues that surface as advocacy issues as well as facilitating informed participation by the public on these issues.

1.3. Protect the confidentiality of all information obtained in the course of professional service. Disclose only information that is directly relevant or necessary to achieve the purpose of disclosure. Release information only with valid consent from a patient or a person legally authorized to consent on behalf of a patient or as authorized by federal or state regulations. The need-to-know criterion is essential when releasing health information for initial disclosure and all redisclosure activities.

1.4. Promote the obligation to respect privacy by respecting confidential information shared among colleagues, while responding to requests from the legal profession, the media, or other non-healthcare related individuals, during presentations or teaching and in situations that could cause harm to persons.

II. **Put service and the health and welfare of persons before self-interest and conduct themselves in the practice of the profession so as to bring honor to themselves, their peers, and to the health information management profession.**

Health information management professionals shall:

2.1. Act with integrity, behave in a trustworthy manner, elevate service to others above self-interest, and promote high standards of practice in every setting.

2.2. Be aware of the profession's mission, values, and ethical principles, and practice in a manner consistent with them by acting honestly and responsibly.

2.3. Anticipate, clarify, and avoid any conflict of interest, to all parties concerned, when dealing with consumers, consulting with competitors, or in providing services requiring potentially conflicting roles (for example, finding out information about one facility that would help a competitor). The conflicting roles or responsibilities must be clarified and appropriate action must be taken to minimize any conflict of interest.

2.4. Ensure that the working environment is consistent and encourages compliance with the AHIMA Code of Ethics, taking reasonable steps to eliminate any conditions in their organizations that violate, interfere with, or discourage compliance with the code.

2.5. Take responsibility and credit, including authorship credit, only for work they actually perform or to which they contribute. Honestly acknowledge the work of and the contributions made by others, verbally or written, such as in publication.

Health information management professionals shall *not*:

2.6. Permit their private conduct to interfere with their ability to fulfill their professional responsibilities.

2.7. Take unfair advantage of any professional relationship or exploit others to further their personal, religious, political, or business interests.

III. **Preserve, protect, and secure personal health information in any form or medium and hold in the highest regards the contents of the records and other information of a confidential nature obtained in the official capacity, taking into account the applicable statutes and regulations.**

Health information management professionals shall:

3.1. Protect the confidentiality of patients' written and electronic records and other sensitive information. Take reasonable steps to ensure that patients' records are stored in a secure location and that patients' records are not available to others who are not authorized to have access.

3.2. Take precautions to ensure and maintain the confidentiality of information transmitted, transferred, or disposed of in the event of a termination, incapacitation, or death of a healthcare provider to other parties through the use of any media. Avoid disclosure of identifying information whenever possible.

3.3. Inform recipients of the limitations and risks associated with providing services via electronic media (such as computer, telephone, fax, radio, and television).

IV. **Refuse to participate in or conceal unethical practices or procedures.**

Health information management professionals shall:

4.1. Act in a professional and ethical manner at all times.

4.2. Take adequate measures to discourage, prevent, expose, and correct the unethical conduct of colleagues.

4.3. Be knowledgeable about established policies and procedures for handling concerns about colleagues' unethical behavior. These include policies and procedures created by AHIMA, licensing and regulatory bodies, employers, supervisors, agencies, and other professional organizations.

4.4. Seek resolution if there is a belief that a colleague has acted unethically or if there is a belief of incompetence or impairment, by discussing their concerns with the colleague when feasible and when such discussion is likely to be productive. Take action through appropriate formal channels, such as contacting an accreditation or regulatory body and/or the AHIMA Professional Ethics Committee.

4.5. Consult with a colleague when feasible and assist the colleague in taking remedial action when there is direct knowledge of a health information management colleague's incompetence or impairment.

Health information management professionals shall *not*:

4.6. Participate in, condone, or be associated with dishonesty, fraud and abuse, or deception. A non-inclusive list of examples includes:

- Allowing patterns of retrospective documentation to avoid suspension or increase reimbursement

- Assigning codes without physician documentation

- Coding when documentation does not justify the procedures that have been billed

- Coding an inappropriate level of service

- Miscoding to avoid conflict with others

- Engaging in negligent coding practices

- Hiding or ignoring review outcomes, such as performance data

- Failing to report licensure status for a physician through the appropriate channels

- Recording inaccurate data for accreditation purposes

- Hiding incomplete medical records
- Allowing inappropriate access to genetic, adoption, or behavioral health information
- Misusing sensitive information about a competitor
- Violating the privacy of individuals

V. Advance health information management knowledge and practice through continuing education, research, publications, and presentations.

Health information management professionals shall:

5.1. Develop and enhance continually their professional expertise, knowledge, and skills (including appropriate education, research, training, consultation, and supervision). Contribute to the knowledge base of health information management and share with colleagues their knowledge related to practice, research, and ethics.

5.2. Base practice decisions on recognized knowledge, including empirically based knowledge relevant to health information management and health information management ethics.

5.3. Contribute time and professional expertise to activities that promote respect for the value, integrity, and competence of the health information management profession. These activities may include teaching, research, consultation, service, legislative testimony, presentations in the community, and participation in professional organizations.

5.4. Engage in evaluation or research that ensures the anonymity or confidentiality of participants and of the data obtained from them by following guidelines developed for the participants in consultation with appropriate institutional review boards. Report evaluation and research findings accurately and take steps to correct any errors later found in published data using standard publication methods.

5.5. Take reasonable steps to provide or arrange for continuing education and staff development, addressing current knowledge and emerging developments related to health information management practice and ethics.

Health information management professionals shall *not*:

5.6. Design or conduct evaluation or research that is in conflict with applicable federal or state laws.

5.7. Participate in, condone, or be associated with fraud or abuse.

VI. Recruit and mentor students, peers, and colleagues to develop and strengthen the professional workforce.

Health information management professionals shall:

6.1. Evaluate students' performance in a manner that is fair and respectful when functioning as educators or clinical internship supervisors.

6.2. Be responsible for setting clear, appropriate, and culturally sensitive boundaries for students.

6.3. Be a mentor for students, peers, and new health information management professionals to develop and strengthen skills.

6.4. Provide directed practice opportunities for students.

Health information management professionals shall *not*:

6.5. Engage in any relationship with students in which there is a risk of exploitation or potential harm to the student.

VII. Accurately represent the profession to the public.

Health information management professionals shall:

7.1 Be an advocate for the profession in all settings and participate in activities that promote and explain the mission, values, and principles of the profession to the public.

VIII. Perform honorably health information management association responsibilities, either appointed or elected, and preserve the confidentiality of any privileged information made known in any official capacity.

Health information management professionals shall:

8.1. Perform responsibly all duties as assigned by the professional association.

8.2. Resign from an Association position if unable to perform the assigned responsibilities with competence.

8.3. Speak on behalf of professional health information management organizations, accurately representing the official and authorized positions of the organizations.

IX. State truthfully and accurately their credentials, professional education, and experiences.

Health information management professionals shall:

9.1. Make clear distinctions between statements made and actions engaged in as a private individual and as a representative of the health information management profession, a professional health information organization, or the health information management professional's employer.

9.2. Claim and ensure that they accurately represent their professional qualifications, credentials, education, competence, affiliations, services provided, training, certification, consultation received, supervised experience, and other relevant professional experience to patients, agencies, and the public.

9.3. Claim only those relevant professional credentials actually possessed and correct any inaccuracies that occur regarding credentials.

X. Facilitate interdisciplinary collaboration in situations supporting health information practice.

Health information management professionals shall:

10.1. Participate in and contribute to decisions that affect the well-being of patients by drawing on the perspectives, values, and experiences of those involved in decisions related to patients. Clearly establish professional and ethical obligations of the interdisciplinary team as a whole and of its individual members.

XI. Respect the inherent dignity and worth of every person.

Health information management professionals shall:

11.1. Treat each person in a respectful fashion, being mindful of individual differences and cultural and ethnic diversity.

11.2. Promote the value of self-determination for each individual.[1]

Reference

[1]American Health Information Management Association Code of Ethics. American Health Information Management Association, July 1, 2004. Available at http://library.ahima.org/xpedio/groups/public/documents/ahima/pub_bok1_024277.html. Accessed October 1, 2004.

Uniform Billing Revenue Codes

How Hospitals Group their Charges

The UB-92 CMS-1450 claim form used by hospitals to bill third-party payers necessitates the use of revenue codes to group like categories of charges. These are three-digit codes that describe all possible categories of hospital, home health, ambulance, or other facility charges. Most claims are submitted using revenue codes at the "zero" or "sum" level, which means using codes ending in zero, which are broader categories than using the full three digits for more detail. Individual payers may require third-digit detail for specific categories. An example of the level of detail is category 110, room and board, private, where the third digit of the code is available to indicate different room types, such as 112–OB private, 113-peds private, 114-psychiatric, private, and others.

Accommodation Revenue Codes

100	All inclusive rate
110	Room and board, private
120	Room and board, semi-private two bed
130	Room and board, semi-private three or four beds
140	Private, deluxe

150	Room and board, ward, five or more beds
160	Other room and board (sterile environment, self-care)
170	Nursery
180	Leave of absence
190	Subacute care
200	Intensive care
210	Coronary care

Ancillary Revenue Codes

220	Special charges
230	Incremental nursing charge rate
240	All inclusive ancillary
250	Pharmacy
260	IV therapy
270	Medical/surgical supplies
280	Oncology
290	Durable medical equipment
300	Laboratory
310	Laboratory pathological
320	Radiology diagnostic
330	Radiology therapeutic
340	Nuclear medicine
350	CT scans
360	Operating room services
370	Anesthesia
380	Blood
390	Blood storage and processing
400	Other imaging services (mammography, ultrasound)
410	Respiratory services
420	Physical therapy
430	Occupational therapy
440	Speech-language pathology
450	Emergency room
460	Pulmonary function
470	Audiology
480	Cardiology
490	Ambulatory surgical care
500	Outpatient services
510	Clinic
520	Free-standing clinic

530	Osteopathic services
540	Ambulance
550	Skilled nursing
560	Medical social services
570	Home health aide
580	Other home health visits
590	Home health units of service
600	Home health oxygen
610	MRI or MRA (magnetic resonance imaging/angiography)
620	Medical / surgical supplies (extension of 270)
630	Pharmacy (extension of 250)
640	Home IV therapy services
650	Hospice services
660	Respite care by home health agency
670	Outpatient special residence charges
700	Cast room
710	Recovery room
720	Labor and delivery room
730	Electrocardiogram (EKG/ECG)
740	Electroencephalogram (EEG)
750	Gastro-intestinal services
760	Treatment or observation room
770	Preventive care services (administration of vaccines)
780	Telemedicine
790	Lithotripsy
800	Inpatient renal dialysis
810	Organ acquisition
820	Hemodialysis, outpatient or home
830	Peritoneal dialysis, ourpatient or home
840	Continuous ambulatory peritoneal dialysis, outpatient
850	Continuous cycling peritoneal dialysis, outpatient
880	Miscellaneour dialysis
900	Psychiatric / psychological treatments
910	Psychiatric / psychological services
920	Other diagnostic services
930	Medical rehabilitation day program
940	Other therapeutic services
960	Professional fees
970	Professional fees
980	Professional fees
990	Patient convenience items[1]

Reference

[1]Medicare Hospital Manual. Pub.10. Chapter 4, Section 460.
Available at: http://www.cms.hhs.gov/manuals/10_hospital/ho460.asp#_460_0.
  Accessed October 3, 2004.

Remittance Advice Reason Codes

Tell Me Why

These codes appear on the remittance advice received by your doctor, to tell him why his claim for services he provided to you has been rejected and not paid. The rejection reason can affect whether or not it is appropriate for him to bill you instead. The reason codes may also appear on the "explanation of benefits" (EOB) you receive. This table explains some of the most commonly used reason codes and the rejection categories they represent:

Code	Description	Category
4	Procedure code inconsistent with modifier or modifier missing	Modifiers
5	Procedure code or bill type inconsistent with place of service	Place of service
6	Procedure / revenue code inconsistent with patient's age	Patient age
7	Procedure / revenue code inconsistent with patient's gender	Patient gender
8	Procedure code inconsistent with provider specialty	Provider
9	Diagnosis inconsistent with patient age	Patient age

Code	Description	Category
10	Diagnosis inconsistent with patient gender	Patient gender
11	Diagnosis inconsistent with procedure	Medical necessity
12	Diagnosis inconsistent with provider type	Provider
13	Date of death precedes date of service	Date of service
14	Date of birth follows date of service	Date of service
15	Payment adjusted because authorization is missing, invalid, or does not apply to service or provider	Prior authorization
16	Claim lacks information needed for adjudication	Requested information
17	Requested information was not provided or was incomplete or insufficient	Requested information
18	Duplicate claim	Duplicate
19	Claim denied because this is work-related injury/illness	Coverage
20	Claim denied because this injury/illness is covered by the liability carrier	Coverage
24	Charges covered under a capitation agreement	Managed care
26	Expenses incurred prior to coverage	Eligibility
27	Expenses incurred after coverage terminated	Eligibility
29	Time limit for filing has expired	Filing limit
31	Patient cannot be identified as our insured	Eligibility
35	Lifetime benefit maximum reached	Coverage
38	Service not provided or authorized by designated provider	Provider
39	Service denied when pre-authorization was requested	Prior authorization
40	Charges do not meet qualifications for emergent or urgent care	Medical necessity
47	Diagnosis not covered, missing, or invalid	Diagnosis
49	Non-covered service because routine exam or screening procedure	Coverage
50	Non-covered because not deemed a medical necessity	Medical necessity
51	Non-covered because pre-existing condition	Coverage
52	Provider not eligible to perform the service billed	Provider
55	Procedure deemed experimental or investigational	Coverage
58	Procedure performed in an inappropriate or invalid place of service	Place of service

Code	Description	Category
59	Charges adjusted based on multiple surgery or concurrent anesthesia rules	Information only
60	Outpatient services with this proximity to inpatient services are not covered	Coverage
62	Payment denied/reduced for absence of prior authorization	Prior authorization
65	Procedure code incorrect	Procedure
96	Non-covered charges	Coverage
97	Payment included in allowance for another service / procedure	Bundling
100	Payment made to patient / insured	Information only
107	Related or qualifying service not previously paid or identified on this claim	Procedure
109	Not covered by this payer. Send claim to correct payer	Eligibility
110	Billing date pre-dates service date	Date of service
113	Service provided ourside the U.S.	Coverage
114	Procedure / product not approved by the Food & Drug Administration	Coverage
115	Procedure postponed or canceled	Information only
116	Advance notice signed by patient did not meet requirements	Medical necessity
117	Transportation only covered to the closest facility	Coverage
119	Benefit maximum reached	Coverage
122	Psychiatric reduction	Information only
126	Deductible	Patient liability
127	Coinsurance	Patient liability
133	Claim pended for further review	Information only
140	Health insurance number and name do not match	Eligibility
146	Diagnosis invalid for date of service	Diagnosis
149	Lifetime benefit reached	Coverage
150	Information submitted does not support this level of service	Medical necessity
151	Information submitted does not support this many services	Medical necessity
152	Information submitted does not support this length of service	Medical necessity
153	Information submitted does not support this dosage	Medical necessity
154	Information submitted does not support this day's supply	Medical necessity

Code	Description	Category
155	Patient refused the service	Information only
157	Service provided as a result of an act of war	Coverage
158	Service provided outside the United States	Coverage
159	Service provided as a result of terrorism	Coverage
160	Injury / illness was the result of an activity that is a benefit exclusion	Coverage
163	Attachment referenced on the claim was not received	Information only
164	Attachment referenced on the claim not received in a timely manner	Information only
A6	Prior hospitalization or 30 day transfer requirement not met	Coverage
A8	Ungroupable DRG	Information only
B1	Noncovered visits	Coverage
B6	Payment adjusted when performed by this type of provider, by this type of provider in this type of facility, or by a provider of this specialty	Provider
B7	Provider not certified / eligible to be paid for this service on this date of service	Provider
B8	Alternative services were available and should have been used	Medical necessity
B9	Not covered because patient is enrolled in a hospice	Coverage
B12	Services not documented in patient's medical record	Information only
B13	Previously paid	Duplicate claim
B14	Only one visit or consultation per physician per day is covered	Coverage
B15	This procedure not paid separately	Bundling
B16	New patient qualification not met	Coding
B18	Procedure code or modifier not valid on date of service	Modifiers
B22	Payment adjusted based on the diagnosis	Diagnosis

Payment System Reference

The payment methodology for Medicare claims is often followed by other payers soon after Medicare implementation. This appendix is intended to be used as a supplement to Chapter 4, to describe the payment methodologies used by different types of facilities or providers. See Chapter 4 for additional information.

Type of provider or facility or service	Payment method and rate
Ambulance	Ambulance fee schedule
Ambulatory Surgery Center (ASC)	ASC payment groups (9)
Cancer Hospital	Reasonable cost
Certified Nurse Midwife	100% of physician fee schedule if billing independently
Clinical Nurse Specialist	65% of physician fee schedule if billing independently
Clinical Psychologist	100% of physician fee schedule. Limited range of services.
Certified Registered Nurse Anesthetist (CRNA)	Anesthetist fee based on anesthesia base and time units
Clinical social worker	75% of physician fee schedule
Comprehensive Outpatient Rehab Facility (CORF)	Combination of prospective payment and fee schedule
Community Mental health Center	Outpatient prospective payment (APC) for partial hospitalization
Critical Access Hospital	Reasonable cost rule

Type of provider or facility or service	Payment method and rate
Durable Medical Equipment (DME)	Fee schedule
End-stage Renal Disease Facility (ESRD)	Composite fee schedule
Federally Qualified Health Center (FQHC)	Reasonable cost rule
Home Health Agency (HHA)	Prospective payment—home health
Hospice	Reasonable cost rules
Hospital Inpatient	Prospective Payment—Diagnosis Related Groups (DRG)
Hospital Outpatient	Prospective payment—Ambulatory Payment Classification (APC)
Hospital Outpatient Lab	Laboratory fee schedule
Hospital Outpatient Occupational Therapy	Fee schedule
Hospital Outpatient Physical Therapy	Physical therapy fee schedule
Hospital Outpatient Speech Therapy	Fee schedule
Independent Diagnostic Testing Facility	Fee schedule
Inpatient Psychiatric	Reasonable cost rules
Inpatient Rehab	Reasonable cost rules
Inpatient Skilled Nursing	Prospective payment—SNF
Nurse Practitioners	85% of physician fee schedule if billing independently
Nursing home intermediate care	Covered by Medicaid—system varies from state to state
Nursing home skilled care	Prospective payment—Resource Utilization Groups (RUGS)
Occupational therapy (private practice)	Fee schedule
Physical therapy (private practice)	Fee schedule
Physician assistant	85% if billing under own number with physician supervision
Physician services	Physician fee schedule or capitation for managed care
Rural health clinic	Reasonable cost rules

Useful Websites

These websites may be useful in your search for additional information about coding, healthcare billing and reimbursement, fraud, and abuse.

Centers for Medicare and Medicaid Services (CMS)

http://www.cms.gov

This federal agency, part of the U.S. Department of Health and Human Services, is responsible for administering the Medicare and Medicaid programs. The website contains information about each program, information for professionals and consumers, and links to hundreds of other websites related to CMS programs.

Statehealthfacts.org

http://www.statehealthfacts.org

This website is operated by the Kaiser Family Foundation. It contains information about health programs in each state, along with data ranking state programs.

American Health Information Management Association (AHIMA)

http://www.ahima.org

AHIMA is the national professional organization for individuals in the health information management field. Its members work in a variety of healthcare settings and perform a variety of functions, from coding to information department management. The website also contains information about health information management educational programs and credentials.

American Academy of Professional Coders (AAPC)

http://www.aapc.com

AAPC represents almost 30,000 individuals nationwide who are involved in the medical coding profession. The website includes information about AAPC educational programs and credentials.

National Center for Health Statistics

http://www.cdc.gov/nchs/

A wealth of information is available on this website about ICD-9-CM and ICD-10-CM, including the official coding and sequencing guidelines.

American Medical Association

http://www.ama-assn.org

As the owner of Current Procedural Terminology (CPT), the American Medical Association controls access to CPT files and data. Their website includes information about how CPT is formulated, and CPT resources available for purchase.

Medical Insurance Bureau

http://www.mib.com

The consumer section of the Medical Insurance Bureau (MIB) informs you what type of files are maintained on individuals, and also provides information on how to order your file.

Uniform Hospital Discharge Data Set

The Uniform Hospital Discharge Data Set (UHDDS) originally developed and adopted in 1974 by the U.S. Department of Health, Education and Welfare, was revised in 1984 and implemented for federal health programs on January 1, 1986.[1] Its purpose is to standardize definitions used in abstracting hospital inpatient data.

The current UHDDS consists of:

1. <u>Personal Identification:</u> The unique number assigned to each patient within a hospital that distinguishes the patient and his or her hospital record from all others in that institution.
2. <u>Date of Birth:</u> Month, day, and year of birth.
3. <u>Sex:</u> Male or female.
4. a. <u>Race:</u>
   White
   Black
   Asian or Pacific Islander
   American Indian / Eskimo / Aleut
   Other

4. b. <u>Ethnicity:</u>

   Spanish origin / Hispanic

   Non-Spanish origin / Non-Hispanic

5. <u>Residence:</u>

   Zip code

   Code for foreign residence

6. <u>Hospital Identification:</u> A unique institutional number within a data collection system.

7–8. <u>Admission and Discharge Dates:</u> Month, day, and year of both admission and discharge. An inpatient admission begins with the formal acceptance by a hospital of a patient who is to receive physician, dentist, or allied services while receiving room, board, and continuous nursing services. An inpatient discharge occurs with the termination of the room, board, and continuous nursing services, and the formal release of an inpatient by the hospital.

9–10. <u>Physician Identification:</u> Each physician must have a unique identification number within the hospital. The attending physician and the operating physician (if applicable) are to be identified.

   Attending Physician: The clinician who is primarily and largely responsible for the care of the patient from the beginning of the hospital episode.

   Operating Physician: The clinician who performed the principal procedure (see item 12).

11. <u>Diagnoses:</u> All diagnoses that affect the current hospital stay.

   Principal Diagnosis: The condition established after study to be chiefly responsible for occasioning the admission of the patient to the hospital for care.

   Other Diagnoses: All conditions that coexist at the time of admission, that develop subsequently, or that affect the treatment received and/or length of stay. Diagnoses that relate to an earlier episode which have no bearing on the current hospital stay are to be excluded.

12. <u>Procedure and Date:</u> All significant procedures are to be reported.

    A significant procedure is one that is surgical in nature, or carries a procedural risk, or carries an anesthetic risk, or requires specialized training. For significant procedures, the identity (by unique number within the hospital) of the person performing the procedure and the date must be reported.

    When more than one procedure is reported, the principal procedure is to be designated. In determining which of several procedures is principal, the following criteria apply:

    The principal procedure is one that was performed for definitive treatment, rather than one performed for diagnostic or exploratory purposes, or was necessary to take care of a complication. If there appears to be two procedures that are principal, then the one most related to the principal diagnosis should be selected as the principal procedure.

    Surgery includes incision, excision, amputation, introduction, endoscopy, repair, destruction, suture, and manipulation.

13. <u>Disposition of Patient:</u>

    Discharged to home

    Left against medical advice

    Discharged to another short-term hospital

    Discharged to a long-term care institution

    Died

    Other

14. <u>Expected payer for most of this bill:</u> The single major source that the patient expects will pay for his or her bill.

Reference

[1]Uniform Hospital Abstract: Minimum Basic Data Set. U.S. Department of Health, Education, and Welfare. Public Health Service. DHEW Publication No. (HRA) 76-1451. Available at: http://www.cdc.gov/nchs/data/series/sr_04/sr04_014.pdf. Accessed February 6, 2005.

JUST AROUND THE CORNER: ICD-10 IS COMING!

Background

The long-awaited mandate that ICD-10-CM/PCS be used for healthcare claims was published in the Federal Register on January 16, 2009. It provided more than four years' lead time to prepare physicians, coders, healthcare facilities and payers to use the new systems. October 1, 2013 is the go-live date for these changes.

The new systems are much more specific than ICD-9-CM, providing better data for:

- Processing claims
- Making informed clinical decisions
- Conducting research
- Tracking public health risks and prevention
- Measuring quality of care provided to patients

- Designing payment systems
- Monitoring health resource utilization

ICD-10-CM is the diagnosis classification system used in all healthcare settings by all types of providers. It was developed by the Centers for Disease Control and Prevention as a clinical modification (CM) of the ICD-10 system used throughout the world. Other countries, such as Canada and Australia, have their own modifications of the international standard code set. Differences between ICD-9-CM and ICD-10-CM can be summarized as follows:

ICD-9-CM Diagnosis Codes	ICD-10-CM Diagnosis Codes
Approximately 14,500 diagnosis codes	Approximately 69,000 diagnosis codes
Valid codes have 3-5 digits	Valid codes have 3-7 digits
Decimal used after third character	Decimal used after third character
First digit is alpha(E or V only) or numeric	First digit is alpha
Digits 2-5 are numeric	Digit 2 is numeric. Digits 3-7 are alphanumeric
Laterality not addressed	Separate codes for laterality (left, right, bilateral) where appropriate
Initial vs. subsequent encounters not addressed	Separate codes for initial and subsequent in some chapters
Combination codes for commonly associated conditions are limited	Many combination codes available
Injuries grouped by type of injury	Injuries grouped by anatomic site
Some clinical concepts not represented, such as underdosing, blood alcohol level	Additional concepts available

ICD-10-PCS is the classification system used by hospitals to code inpatient procedures. These procedure codes are used only in the United States. They were developed by 3M under contract with the Center for Medicare and Medicaid Services (CMS) as a replacement for the outdated ICD-9-CM Procedure Codes. Because ICD-9 procedure codes had only 4 digits, the system was severely limited in its ability to accommodate new technology and advances in surgical techniques. ICD-10-PCS is dramatically different in methodology, utilizing the "root operation" concept, which describes the objective of the procedure. Other differences between ICD-9 Procedure Codes and ICD-10-PCS are as follows:

ICD-9-CM Procedure Codes	ICD-10-PCS Procedure Codes
Approximately 4,000 procedure codes	Approximately 72,000 procedure codes
Valid codes have 4 digits, all numeric	Valid codes all have 7 alphanumeric characters (the letters O and I are not used, to avoid confusion with zero and one)
Decimal used after second digit	No decimals used
Procedure codes often contained diagnostic concepts	Procedure codes are descriptive of the body system, body part, root operation, approach, devices and certain additional qualifying characters. No diagnostic information is included.
Eponymic (named after a person) terms were common	No eponyms
Coding process involved finding procedure in the index and verifying in the tabular lists	Coding process is directly from body system/ root operation tables. Each row in a table defines valid combinations of code values

Official guidelines will be used to govern both ICD-10-CM diagnosis coding and ICD-10-PCS procedure coding.

CMS has also published General Equivalence Mappings (GEMs) that can be used to convert coded data from 9 to 10 and vice versa.

Mappings are available for both diagnosis and procedure code sets. These should not be considered as a substitute for learning and using ICD-10 because in many cases, there is not a direct one-to-one mapping, so the code-to-code correspondence is only approximate. Most of the time, there will be more codes in ICD-10 because it is much more specific. The GEMs can be useful in converting historical ICD-9 data to ICD-10 for comparison purposes.

CPT will continue to be used for physician billing and hospital outpatient procedures.

New Coding System Challenges and Costs

Although many free resources are available to help providers and facilities make the transition to ICD-10, there will definitely be some costs associated with the change:

Training: in addition to providers and coders, many other healthcare staff need to be familiar with the new systems and understand how they work. Whether or not PCS is included in the training will depend on the type of facility.

Target Group	Training needed
Patient access/registration staff	Basic concepts of new systems; effect on prior authorization process and medical necessity documentation
Patient financial services	Basic concepts of relevant systems; impact on payment systems, including fee-for-service and prospective payment such as DRGs
Information technology	Basic concepts of new systems; impact on not only internal systems but also interfaces
	How coding system changes will affect cost reporting, financial reports. How GEMs can be used to assist in historical comparisons

Target Group	Training needed
Accounting and finance	Basic concepts of systems used. This group needs to understand the level of documentation needed to support new codes
Providers and ancillary department staff	Thorough training on systems and documentation; potential use of GEMs to facilitate use of existing databases and reports
Compliance and quality management	Non-coding staff need familiarity with the new systems and impact on HIM processes
Health information management Contracting	Familiarity with systems to assure that all necessary coverage and reimbursement information is present in contracts

Changes to Data Capture Mechanisms: This may include superbills or encounter forms, if the healthcare entity is still using paper. Given the fact that both CM and PCS are much more specific, expanding a paper form may not be practical. The change to ICD-10 may provide in impetus to switch to electronic charge capture because it can be updated and customized more easily. Regardless of which method is used, there will be costs associated with staff time, vendor time, and possible extra printing costs.

Changes to Computer Systems: Modifications to software will need to allow, at a minimum, the expanded number of digits in both ICD-10-CM and ICD-10-PCS. Any system that uses coded data will be affected: practice management systems, electronic health record systems, clinical database warehouses, coding software integrated with ancillary testing equipment, lab data systems, and financial systems using coded data. Although vendors will generally be responsible for software changes in preparation for ICD-10, internal staff time will also be required for verification and testing.

Increased Documentation: This is probably the biggest change related to ICD-10. The lack of specific documentation required by the expanded code systems can entail risk for providers and facilities due to medical necessity proof required by payers. Although "unspecified" codes will continue to be present in ICD-10-CM, payers may require specific codes before they reimburse. The use of unspecified codes could result in rejected claims or claim suspension pending the receipt of documentation to support the codes billed.

Business Process Analysis: In order to determine how the change to ICD-10-CM and PCS will affect current processes, it is necessary to clearly document what those are. This will require staff or outside consultant time and effort. Once the current process is understood, all of the potential impact points of the change to ICD-10-CM and PCS should be defined and analyzed.

Reduction in Productivity: Productivity will suffer before, during and after code change implementation. Staff and providers who are in training are not seeing patients and generating bills. Increased documentation needs and unfamiliarity with the new systems can affect provider throughput and coder productivity. After implementation, ongoing monitoring will be needed to assure all systems are working properly with the new codes.

Cash Flow Concerns: Payers who are also adapting to the new coding systems may experience slowdowns in processing and paying claims. As a number of current payment methodologies are tied directly to procedure and/or diagnosis codes, new algorithms containing the new codes may work differently, affecting reimbursement rates.

Strategies for Successful Implementation

No matter the size of the healthcare practice or facility, successful implementation of ICD-10-CM and ICD-10-PCS (inpatient hospital) requires careful planning and organization. It is not possible to flip the switch on October 1, 2013 if systems are not already in place to handle the new codes. In smaller practices, the transition plan will likely be handled by existing staff, while outside vendors or consultants may be needed to assist larger groups or facilities.

Key tasks to perform are:

1. Inform providers and staff about the coding systems changes.
    - Posters, e-mails, flyers about what is coming, why, and when

2. Organize the implementation project
    - Identify a project manager or owner
    - Identify key staff to participate in steering committee to oversee project
    - Establish timeline and meeting schedule
    - Coordinate a plan for communicating project information and issues to the organization
    - Start preliminary budget projections for implementation costs

3. Evaluate current processes that use coding
    - Identify all work processes that use ICD-9
    - Identify current electronic systems that use ICD-9
    - Identify staff who use ICD-9
    - Assess the potential impact of ICD-10 on all current processes

4. Assess readiness of vendors to implement ICD-10 within mandated timeframes
    - Determine if new hardware will be needed to support updated systems
    - Ask about timeframes for updates and installation that allow for testing prior to the go-live date

5. Plan and Implement Staff Training
   - Identify who needs which training, based on roles within the organization
   - Determine methods, budget and time needed for training
   - Purchase or develop training materials
   - Identify certified individuals who will conduct training

6. Conduct a gap analysis of provider documentation
   - Once coders are trained, look at samples of provider documentation to determine adequacy for supporting ICD-10 codes
   - Use outcomes of gap analysis to provide additional provider feedback and training

7. Manage contractual changes
   - Review payer contracts and collaborate to determine how they might be modified as a result of code changes
   - Contact payers for information about reimbursement schedules using the new code sets

8. Evaluate the effect on historical data
   - Are there existing code databases that will require conversion to make them comparable with new data under ICD-10?

9. Develop strategic plans to reduce provider and coder productivity decreases
   - Will additional coders or computer-assisted coding systems be needed to supplement existing staff during the go-live period
   - Is it anticipated that reductions in cash flow will require supplemental financing during the implementation period?

10. Conduct internal and external testing of new and upgraded systems
    - Assure that systems and vendors can handle new codes
    - Review results of testing and make necessary changes to systems

11. Go-live ! October 1, 2013

12. Monitor claims and reimbursement for at least 3-6 months
    - Assure that appropriate reimbursement is occurring
    - Conduct documentation audits to assure that new codes being billed are supported by provider documentation

ICD-10 Implementation Resources:

Centers for Medicare and Medicaid Services (CMS)
https://www.cms.gov/ICD10/

American Health Information Management Association (AHIMA)
http://www.ahima.org/icd10/

American Academy of Professional Coders (AAPC)
http://www.aapc.com/ICD-10/

American Medical Association
http://www.ama-assn.org/ama/pub/physician-resources/solutions-managing-your-practice/coding-billing-insurance/hipaahealth-insurance-portability-accountability-act/transaction-code-set-standards/icd10-code-set.page

Many other medical specialty societies or ancillary provider organizations also have ICD-10 information and implementation resources on their websites.

Index